NEY MATTERS 101 SERIES

PAGES OF

RMS AND TEMPLATES INCLUDED

ORGANIZE YOUR CHURCH FOR PURPOSE:

A Comprehensive Management & Financial Planning Guide for Church Administrators & Pastors

More books in the Money Matters 101 Series:

Organizing Your Church for Purpose:
A Comprehensive Management and Financial Planning Guide for Church Administrators and Pastors

(Money Matters 101 Series)

ISBN-13: 978-1974588947
ISBN-10: 1974588947

http://DanetteONealPublishing.com

To my parents Silas & Beulah O'Neal, I live to make you proud.
Thank you WEOP for the inspiration and opportunities to grow.

I thank God for His Grace, and His anointing for Kingdom building.

PREFACE
HOW TO USE THIS GUIDE

This guide was developed by Dr. Danette O'Neal out of more than 30 years experience as a Real Estate Broker and Ministry Advisor to Senior Pastors and their Administrators. The tutorials, guides, templates, and sample worksheets will help you meet any financial institution's requirements for lending, increase accountability and membership, fundraising, and move your congregation to spiritual and financial sustainability.

The "good ole boy" system does not have a place in today's church. With a lack of integrity prevelant in the marketplace, the church needs to stand fast in managing its finances. I have found that creating detailed financial reports can be difficult, and becomes secondary when a Pastor is busy trying to run a church with volunteers. Gathering the information for these financial reports are a balancing act; however, it becomes a really big deal when the church experiences a loss, applies for a loan, or when preparing for an annual meeting with the membership.

Churches are now under more scrutiny from the IRS and banking institutions as the rate of foreclosures has drastically increased in the last decade. Just because your church has been granted tax-exempt status doesn't mean it is not held accountable by both the government and by community that it serves.

Last, the most practical use for this book is that it will guide you to managing the sacred donations to your church, and show respect for those who sacrifice so much to give to your church by keeping track of your finances. Church administrators and board members will be able to use this collective information to build financial statements, make responsible decisions, and apply for government grants to expand its mission.

Respectfully,

Dr. Danette O'Neal

ABOUT THE AUTHOR:

DR.
DANETTE
O'NEAL

http://danetteoneal.com

Facebook@danetteoneal
Twitter@danetteoneal
Linkedin@danetteoneal
Instagram@danetteoneal

Dr. Danette O'Neal, Author-LEED educator, HGTV alumna, entrepreneur, and trainer is the Broker/Owner of Danette O'Neal Realtors (DOR) with offices in the Greater New Orleans and Atlanta Metro areas.

Dr. O'Neal specializes in residential and commercial sales, property management and spiritual architecture. With more than 28 years in real estate, she regularly lends her expertise to nonprofit organizations to expand their missions by lecturing on financial fitness, entrepreneurial training, and consulting for organizational leadership and sustainability. Her focus is on supporting organizations to grow through engaging their people with executive and business coaching, strategic planning and the facilitation of a range of leadership development programs.

She holds a PhD in Public Policy and Administration, a Masters in Public Administration both from Walden University, and a M.A. in Community Economic Development from Southern New Hampshire University. She is a Professor and SME for Strayer and Realtor Universities in the Schools of Business, Real Estate, and Public Administration. Dr. O'Neal is the 2017 Chair of the Professional Development Committee and serves on the Convention Committee for the National Association of Realtors. She volunteers as an interpreter for the deaf and is a leader in the Full Gospel Baptist Church International Hearing Impaired Ministry.

Table of Contents

SAMPLE FORMS AND TEMPLATES

GETTING STARTED:
HOW WELL DO YOUR KNOW YOUR ORGANIZATION

NAME OF ORGANIZATION	
ADDRESS OF ORGANIZATION	
PHONE NUMBERS	
MAIN CONTACT (S)	
WHAT IS THE LEGALSTRUCTURE?	
STATE (S) OF INCORPORTION	

TAX I.D # /EIN	
NAME, ADDRESS, PH # OF LAW FIRM REPRESENTAITON	
NAME, ADDRESS, PH# OF CPA FIRM REPRESENTATION	
WHAT IS THE LEGALSTRUCTURE?	
STATE (S) OF INCORPORTION	

Inception date of Organization	
How long have you been at your location?	
How long at the previous location?	
How many worship services weekly	

Mission of Organization

(The Church Mission Statement is very practical in its scope. In other words, it focuses on what your church will accomplish and how it will accomplish it).

Vision of Organization

(Vision Statement is more designed to be abstract. In other words, it focuses on the personality of the church and how God sees your local church fitting into the larger framework of the global church).

Goals

(These goals are steps your church would take to achieve a strategic objective. The goals for your church should always be realistic, specific, measurable, attainable, and timely. Example: To have at least 50% of the congregation actively involved in at least one ministry away from the church property that is "meeting people, meeting needs, meeting Christ". These goals could be anything).

Objectives of Organization

SEE (4 PG.) SAMPLE MISSION, VISION, AND GOALS WORKSHEET IN FORMS SECTION

PREPARING THE SWOT ANALYSIS

SWOT Analysis Template

State what you are assessing here

(This particular example is for a new business opportunity. Many criteria can apply to more than one quadrant. Identify criteria appropriate too your own SWOT situation.)

Strengths

Criteria examples
Advantages of proposition
Capabilities
Competitive advantages
USP's (unique selling points)
Resources, Assets, People
Experience, knowledge, data
Financial reserves, likely returns
Marketing - reach, distribution, awareness
Innovative aspects
Location and geographical
Price, value, quality
Accreditations, qualifications, certifications
Processes, systems, IT, communications

Weaknesses

Criteria examples
Disadvantages of proposition
Gaps in capabilities
Lack of competitive strength
Reputation, presence and reach
Financials
Own known vulnerabilities
Timescales, deadlines and pressures
Cash flow, start-up cash-drain
Continuity, supply chain robustness
Effects on core activities, distraction
Reliability of data, plan predictability
Morale, commitment, leadership
Accreditations etc

Opportunities

Criteria examples
Market developments
Competitors' vulnerabilities
Industry or lifestyle trends
Technology development and innovation
Global influences
New markets, vertical, horizontal
Niche target markets
Geographical, export, import
New USP's
Tactics: eg, surprise, major contacts
Business and product development
Information and research
Partnerships, agencies

Threats

Criteria examples
Political effects
Legislative effects
Environmental effects
IT developments
Competitor intentions - various
Market demand
New technologies, services, ideas
Vital contracts and partners
Sustaining internal capabilities
Obstacles faced
Insurmountable weaknesses
Loss of key staff
Sustainable financial backing
Economy - home, abroad
Seasonality, weather effects

ORGANIZATION'S- Strengths

Weaknesses

Opportunities

Threats

HOW WELL DO YOUR KNOW YOUR ORGANIZATION (Part II)

Do you currently own or rent at this location?	
Seating capacity of current facility:	
Senior Pastor or Leader name:	
Length of time with current organization	
Leaders age: Ordained for:	
Names of Associate Pastors, titles/roles, length of time at organization:	

Names of other staff, /clergy, titles/roles, and length of time with the organization:	
Member of Denominational Body Yes/No? If yes, Which one: If yes, how is the body structured? If yes, how much does your organization contribute directly to the denomination annually:	

What forms of financial assistance are available from the denominational body:	

CHURCH LEADERSHIP

What committee/person is in charge of financial related decisions:	
What committee/person is in charge of other decisions:	
What is the leadership term (if any) for persons responsible for decision making:	

INSURANCE

Does the church carry a life insurance policy of the head clergy for which the church is the beneficiary?	
If so what is the amount of the policy?	
What other types of insurance and amounts does the church carry?	
When was the last time the insurance policies were reviewed?	
Who is authorized to make changes?	

Please complete the following chart:

KEY MANAGEMENT COMPOSITION

NAME	TITLE	PROFESSIONAL EXPERIENCE	EDUCATION	AGE

ORGANIZATIONAL STRUCTURE

KEY COMMITTEE	CHAIRPERSON	#OF COMMITTEE MEMERS	TERM	AVERAGE # OF YRS OF COMMITTEE

FINANCIAL INFORMATION & MEMBERSHIP

Record the information for the last 5 years.

Fiscal Yr. Ended	2012	2013	2014	2015	2016
1. Operating budget Amount:					
2. Actual operating Income:					
3. Membership #					
4. # of Giving Units:					
5. Average worship attendance- Sunday services:					

6. What is the average attendance for the primary Sunday Service in this current year: _____

7. Average Sunday School Attendance: _____

8. Average Bible Study attendance

9. **BREAKDOWN OF CURRENT MEMBERSHIP: In (%)**

Under 18	
18-25	
25-35	
35-45	
45-55	
55-65	
Over 65	

(Note: if your organization has a breakdown in alternate age grouping, please use that grouping)

10. When was the last date your membership rolls were purged: _____.

11. Who writes the checks for the organization: _____.

12. Who signs the checks for the organization: _____.

13. Who reconciles the Bank Statements: _____.

14. How does the organization utilize technology in its operations?

How is technology used for financial management?	
How is technology used to track membership?	
How is technology used for contribution monitoring?	

15. What are your average total depository balances per month? _____
_____.

16. How many bank accounts do you have? _____

17. What is the purpose of each account?

BANK	ACCT #	PURPOSE

REAL ESTATE HOLDINGS:
Provide a summary of any real estate owned, capital, or land additions

FACILITY	ACQUISITION DATE	COST	FINANCES	TOTAL SQ FT.	EST. PRESENT VALUE

PROPERTY INFORMATION

1. How many acres do you own: Is the legal description filed in your office?

   _____

2. What is the square footage of your facilities: _____

3. How many acres are occupied by your facilities: _____

4. What date did you acquire your present facility and what was the cost:

   _____.

5. Appraised value of property and improvements, if known: _____

   Date of appraisal: _____.

6. Date and name of surveyor on latest survey:

   _____

7. Do you have owner's title insurance: _____

USE THIS FORM IF YOUR ORGANIZATION IS CURRENTLY SEEKING FINANCING FOR A NEW PROPERTY OR ADDITIONAL PROPERTY:

DESCRIPTION A THE CURRENT PROJECT:		
HOW MUCH IS THE ACQUISTION?		
LAND OR EXISTING STRUCTURE?		
WHO IS THE ARCHITECT?		
WHO IS THE BUILDER?		
WHAT IS THE COST OF THE PROJECT?	Construction	$
	Soft Cost	$
	Furniture/Fixtures	$
	Contingency	$
	Closing Cost	$
	Interest during Construction	$
	Total Estimated Cost	$
Anticipated length of construction:		
How much cash is available for the project today?		

Are you/will you be involved in a special fundraising campaign for the project in progress? _____.

If yes, period during which pledges were/will be taken (mo/yr-mo. yr/)	
If yes, when were payments against pledges to start:	
If yes, what is/was the length of the pledges	
If yes, how much is pledged to date	
If yes, how many dollars have been received from pledges to date:	
If yes, any pledges over $25,000	
Did you use a professional fund-raiser:	
Have you been involved in project fundraising in the past?	

Complete the following chart if you have been involved in a project fundraiser in the past:

past pledge campaigns (most recent 3)

Years			
Term			
Amount Pledge % Collected?			
Professional Fundraiser Y/N			
Purpose			

How many donors contribute more than 10% of the annual operating revenue of the organization? How long has this person been a member?

Briefly describe the organization's plans for capital expenditures, maintenance of operations, additional equipment purchases, and/or new programs and services over the next 3 years.

What are the estimated costs of each of these expenditures/services?

List name and occupation of individuals serving on Committee/Board that makes the financial decisions/recommendation

Operating budget projections and membership/attendance projections for next three years.

What is the target market for membership for your organization?

How does the organization market itself to the community and differentiate itself from other organizations in the community?

What type of advertising campaigns are you currently involved in?

Attach to this binder ….A brief history of the organization

Attach to this binder:

- **The resume of the Senior Pastor, CEO, and CFO**
- **The last three (3) years of fiscal year-end financial statements**
- **The most recent interim financial statement**
- **A copy of the latest budget**

ORGANIZATIONAL STRUCTURE

Dept/ Auxiliary/Committee	Leader	Asst. Leader

The Church's Annual Internal Audit
(see sample templates in forms)

None of us want to ever think that the misuse of church funds or embezzlement could ever happen in our very own church but truth is it can happen. It happens in some churches on a small scale by persons they thought were a trusted employee and volunteers working for the church.

Misuse of church funds can occur when a lack of internal controls or accounting system is in place. You can see now why internal and external audits are very important.

Procedures or forms can be created to track the following departments:

Financial Statements:

- Are monthly financial statements prepared on a timely basis and submitted to the church board or appropriate person or committee?
- Where are they kept?
- Are they reconciled monthly?

Cash Receipts:

- Are cash handling procedures in writing or store in the Cloud?

Donation Records/Receipting:

- Are individual donor records kept as a basis to provide donor acknowledgements for all contributions?
- How is donor confidentiality maintained?

Cash Disbursements:

- Are all disbursements paid by check except for minor expenditures paid through the petty cash fund?
- Is there a tracking system for petty cash?
- Is the petty cash fund periodically reconciled and replenished based on proper documentation of the cash expenditures?

Bank Statement Reconciliation:

- Are written bank reconciliations prepared on a timely basis?
- Are the reconciliations for the last month in the fiscal year.
- Is there a tracing system in place to triangulate transactions between the bank and the books for completeness and timeliness.

Savings and Investment Accounts:

- Are all savings and investment accounts recorded in the financial records?

Land, Buildings, and Equipment Records:

- Are there detailed records of land, buildings and equipment including date acquired, description and cost of fair market value of date of acquisition

Accounts Payable:

- Is there a schedule of unpaid invoices including vendor name, invoice date and due date?

Insurance Policies:

- Is there a schedule of insurance coverage in force? Are these date recorded on an calendar to reflect effective and expiration dates, kind and classification of coverage, maximum amounts of each coverage, premiums and terms of payment.

Amortization of Debt:

- Is there a schedule of debit such as mortgages and notes?

Securities and Other Negotiable Documents:

- Does the organization own any CD's, Money Market accounts or bonds?
- If so, are they kept in a safety deposit box?

Personal Matters:

- *Does the organization maintain the following documents?*
    1. Applications for Employment, W-4 Forms for Each Employee,
    2. Personnel Files, Performance Appraisal and Evaluation Forms,
    3. Employee Handbook and Immigration I-9 Forms

Federal Reporting Obligations:

- Does the organization file on a timely basis

Budget Forms and Formats

(see sample templates in forms)

The church is somewhat like our lives we have to budget in order to not overwhelm the monies. This requires a maximum number of church members to be involved in developing the annual budget. These church members can form a committee to organize a successful budget for their church.

The Budget Request form is to be completed by department and ministry leaders on an annual basis to request funding on the budget for your church. The "How to Plan an Annual Budget" for your church has some great information and a 2 page Church Annual Budget Worksheet that will give you a head start. Click link above to access these forms.

Mission Budgeting Request Form- The Mission Budgeting Request form can be an asset if your church has missionaries and the vision to spread the Gospel of Jesus Christ to the ends of the world. Missions is a very important part of the church, and in these tough and uncertain economic times you certainly will need to budget for this vision. With a budget and special church members with a very special missions vision, this is a very possible vision even in the smallest of churches.

Outreach Project Ideas & Worksheet - is a great tool when your church only has a limited and budgeted amount for mission or outreach activities. This worksheet will track your total outreach budget amount along with all the expenses and then will let you know when the expenses has exceeded your budgeted amount of monies.

Missions is a very important part of the church, and in these tough and uncertain economic times you certainly will need to budget for this vision. With a budget and special church members with a very special missions vision, this is a very possible vision even in the smallest of churches.

CHURCH FUNDRAISING

(see templates in form section)

Does your church have Fundraisers to raise money for special causes? If yes, then you might want these fundraiser forms below to help your church fundraising coordinator to get the proper approvals from administration before and after the fundraising event. The key to a successful fundraising event is to be very well prepared and organized before, during, and after the event. The accounting form for church fundraising should include:

1. **Name of church**
2. **Name of form** - Fundraising Accounting Form
3. **Current date**
4. **Name and date of event**
5. **Event leader and contact information**
6. **Name of organizing group or ministry**
7. **Estimated # of participants/attendees**
8. **Event leader and contact information**
9. **Number of event volunteers needed**
10. **Estimated # of volunteer hours**
11. **Income details** - e.g., ticket sales, food, silent auction, etc. and total income
12. **The estimated value of any non-cash donations** -
13. **Expense details** - e.g., food, equipment rental, supplies, postage, etc. and total expenses
14. **Net event proceeds**- Income minus Expenses
15. **Name of person who completed the form**
16. **Fundraiser monies will be used for**
17. **Explanation of difference between estimate and actual profit**
18. **Approval of fundraiser (before the event)**- Event Organizer's Signature and Date, Department Chair or Club Advisor's Signature and Date, Division Director of Fundraiser Activities Signature and Date
19. **Approval of Actuals (AFTER the event)** - Department Chair or Club Advisor's Signature and Date and Division Director of Fundraiser Activities Signature and Date

Book keeping hint: *ALL deposits for this event should contain the same description as above.*

CHURCH INVENTORY

(see templates in forms section)

Inventory forms for churches such Inventory Count, Inventory Status, Church Inventory List, and Church Property Inventory along with instructions are free to download for your church inventory. The Inventory forms for churches (in the rear section of this binder) helps relieve any doubt as to whether the item in question was given or loaned to the church. Any item marked with a serial number will need to be listed on the forms.

- Office Furniture
- Copy Machine
- Desk
- Chairs
- Pew chairs

It is probably a good idea to have some kind of control over your church property. Here are some suggestions for establishing your own church inventory control:

- Mark each church property with the church name and an inventory control serial number. If you have an item that does not have a serial number then you know that it was most likely loaned to the church. You can use mailing labels to mark the church property and print these labels from your church office computer or typewriter.
- Keep an official listing or database of the church property.
- Have one designated person to keep track of all the church inventory records.
- Stay organized and keep the forms simple.

On of the smartest things your church could ever do is completing a personal property inventory of your church.

In the unexpected event that a disaster strikes and your church files an insurance claim, you might have to provide a church inventory to highlight the damaged items. Think about it, could you list and value the major items in the sanctuary from memory? Could you list the valuables in the church nursery or kitchen? What about the personal property of others that are stored in the church?

If your church suffers a loss, a detailed inventory not only helps you determine adequate amounts of coverage for personal property before a loss, but it also speeds the insurance claim process.

CHURCH BYLAWS

The Church's Bylaws act as the governing documents of a new church or an existing church and are typically originally formulated at the church's foundation. Bylaws act as rules of the organization, laying the groundwork for church elections, leadership, missions, programs, and other important matters. Before writing church bylaws, elect a group of representatives from the community who want to become part of a new congregation or those who are already parishioners.

Tips and Warnings:

- Bylaws can be a method of avoiding crisis situations and can help protect the church from liability. Make sure that they are clearly written.
- If you choose to incorporate as a non-profit organization, it is important to write the bylaws before incorporating with the state or federal government. See Church Bylaws sample below guidelines.

Guidelines to Writing Church Bylaws

1. Meet with the church board to decide your bylaws and determine the focus of your church. The secretary of the board should take minutes for the bylaw meeting.

2. Write the church's official name, bank documents, bills, bank accounts and other pertinent documentation.

3. Define the church's purpose, what you plan to address through your ministries, and your legal status. Is your church a registered tax-exempt non-profit organization or do you have another tax status? This will help you define how you will operate in terms of donations and it's very important. Only non-profit organizations can accept tax-deductible donations.

4. Discuss the denomination of your church, If your church belongs to a specific denomination, it's important that you mention this in your bylaws. This will help guide your church's statement of faith or what your congregation holds to be true.

5. Write your church's mission statement and outline how the leaders of your church plan to achieve its purpose and goals. Will your church focus on outreach projects or programs?

6. Discuss the requirements for membership to your church, including the process of becoming a member and each congregant's right, responsibilities, and requirements for members if any applies. Include whether congregants will have voting rights or if the voting rights are held solely by the board.

7. Define how staff members are chosen or elected and their responsibilities within the congregation. Clearly outline how the choosing or election process will work.

8. Write the rules for board meetings, including who has the right to vote, how the meetings will be regulated, and how often financial updates should occur.

9. Define the departments within your church, such as finance, women's ministry, youth ministry, pro-life or other areas that your church will focus on.

10. Discuss the church's ability to own land and have assets and whose name they will be listed under. A church must abide by state laws. Some states require incorporation in order to own land. If you do not incorporate, then the assets of the church should be placed in one person's name.

11. Explain how your church's bylaws can be amended and if majority vote is required. As the church grows, revisions might need to be made to the bylaws.

12. Plan in case the church might be dissolved and how church assets will be distributed if the church closes.

13. Hold a vote to approve the bylaws. If a majority of the board members approve it, this will be a legally-binding document to guide the church.

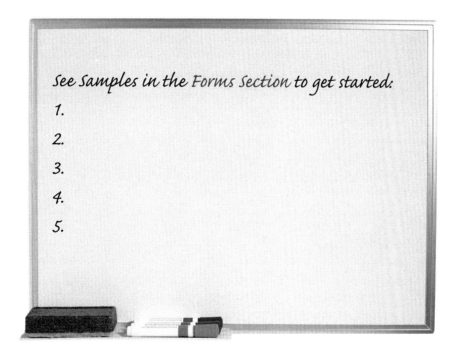

See Samples in the Forms Section to get started:

1.

2.

3.

4.

5.

What is a Church Policy & Procedures Manual?

A Church Policies and Procedures Manual is a reference guide to the functions and operations of the church. It lists routine duties and answers questions that arise as duties are performed. The procedure section gives step-by-step instructions for performing each task.

What Is A Policy?

A Policy is a statement that defines the authority required, boundaries set, responsibilities delegated, and guidelines, established to carry out a function of the church. In other words, **policies** are **"what"** a company does or who does the task, why it is done, and, under what conditions it is done. Policies answer questions that arise during unique circumstances.

Policies provide uniform treatment of a situation, thus achieving continuity of operation. Policies take personalities out of the picture. Decisions are based on the church policy not on the individual, and each situation is treated the same.

What Is A Procedure?

Procedures tell **"how"** a task is done. A detailed listing is made of each step taken to complete the process. A step-by-step description of the process is used to complete the job.

This finish binder can guide you when developing your own church policy and procedures. Policies cover leadership, management, financial, personnel, general administration, and ministry.

Policy and procedures, if properly applied, become very invaluable for identifying and assigning responsibilities, keeping a quality level of performance throughout church ministries, and protecting the congregation and church leaders as a whole.

The church policy and procedures should be kept in a manual available for the church administration to access at any time. If a question arises, the manual should have policies:

Accounting Policy	Bookkeeping Practices	Facilities Usage Policy
Ministry Expense Policy	Building Fund Policy	Finance Committee Practices
Background Check Policy	Church Internet Policy	Missions Policy
Cell Phone Use Policy	Credit Card Usage Policy	Discipline/Probation Policy
Church Bus Usage Policy	Conflict of Interest Policy	Travel Policy
Church Treasurer Policy	Financial Assistance Policy	Safety Policy

The Church Business Plan

(template in forms section)

Do you have a Business Plan for your church? If not, then you can start now with the sample below to help you create your own plan for your church. Strategic planning is a very important part of the creation, development and growth of your church or any other organization. Church business planning allows the ability to map out strategic steps to help your organization achieve their mission and vision.

The Church Business Plans Needs to Include:

- **Mission and Vision Statements** - You need statements to help explain where your church is going and why you want to get there and the principles that guide the organization.
- **Market Research** - This will determine if there is a need for what your church offers in the community. Make sure to get the opinions of the people who live in the community. Provide detailed information about competing churches in your area to find out what they offer and who they appeal to. Provide detailed information on how your church can fill in gaps with ministries to various age groups and community activities.
- **Marketing Plan** - This plan should explain how you will let prospective attendees how about your church and its unique offerings, such as by advertising your worship services, Bible studies and children's activities in the local paper.
- **Management Team** - Explain in detail including their past experience in helping the church grow the management team that will be implementing the plan. If they don't have experience at other churches, describe any other business successes they have achieved. Include a little background information on the people who will be impacting the plan's success, such as the Pastor and Youth Fellowship Leaders.
- **Daily Operation of Church** - Explain in steps the daily operation of your church including the duties of the administrator, minister, staff and volunteers who lead studies or group activities. Describe the church facility where you hold services and classes, and insert costs involved in moving to a larger facility once membership increases. List the equipment you will need over the next few years for the church, and this section should also include the insurance coverage the church carries.
- **Financial Reports** - Provide the church financial information as the final section of the plan including operating budgets, last 3 years of financial statements as well as 3 years of forecasted projections including profit and loss statements. The profit and loss statements need to have all the potential contributions made to the church as well as expenses (Pastor's salary, utilities, rental space, etc.). Also include information on how your church qualifies as a non-profit organization to stay exempt from paying taxes.
- **1-3 Page Executive Summary** - This is the last step but place it at the beginning of the plan. This summary needs to express the most important parts of the plan so that's why it's best to create it after you finish your plan.

SAMPLE CHURCH BUDGET & RECOMMENDED ACCOUNTING CODES

Sample Proposed Church Budget SPREADSHEET

Line#	Acct #	Description	This Year	Last Year	$ Change	% Change	% of 2005 GF total	% of 2005 Grand Total
2		**Staff Wages & Benefits**						
3	5001	Senior Pastor (includes SECA)	$63,900	$62,000	$1,900	3.1%		
4	5002	Pastor 2 (includes SECA)	$42,600	$41,300	$1,300	3.1%		
5	5010	Ministry Staff Wages	138,000	133,800	$4,200	3.1%		
6	5020	Support Staff Wages	83,120	80,000	$3,120	3.9%		
7		**Total Wages**	327,620	317,100	$10,520	3.3%	46.9%	46.6%
8		**Staff Benefits**						
9	5051	Automobile Mileage Reimbursement	4,800	4,000	$800	20.0%		
10	5052	Health Insurance	42,402	38,000	$4,402	11.6%		
11	5053	Ministers Pension Fund	10,576	10,000	$576	5.8%		
12	5054	Pastor/Staff Training	9,000	6,000	$3,000	50.0%		
13	5055	Payroll Taxes	16,736	15,000	$1,736	11.6%		
14	5056	Workers Compensation	2,310	2,250	$60	2.7%		
15	5057	403B Match	3,000	3,000	$0	0.0%		
16	5058	Sabbatical Fund	2,000	2,000	$0	0.0%		
17		**Total Benefits**	90,824	80,250	$10,574	13.2%	13.0%	12.9%
18		**Total Staff Wages & Benefits**	418,444	397,350	$21,094	5.3%	59.9%	59.5%
19								
20		**Worship/Music**						
21	6010	Audio/Visual/Equipment	1,000	1,000	$0	0.0%		
22	6015	Drama Ministry	1,000	1,000	$0	0.0%		
23	6020	Music License	1,000	1,000	$0	0.0%		
24	6025	Musicians - Contract Labor	1,000	1,000	$0	0.0%		
25	6030	Pulpit Supply	1,000	1,000	$0	0.0%		
26	6040	Refreshments / Hospitality	1,000	1,000	$0	0.0%		
27	6050	Rent - Worship/Music	1,000	1,000	$0	0.0%		
28	6060	Special Music	1,000	1,000	$0	0.0%		

PURPOSE CHURCH BUDGET SPREEDSHEET (PAGE 2.)

#	Code	Name					
29	6070	Supplies	1,000	1,000	$0	0.0%	
30	6080	Training	1,000	1,000	$0	0.0%	
31		**Total Worship/Music**	**10,000**	**10,000**	**$0**	**0.0%**	1.4% / 1.4%
32							
33		**Pastoral Care**					
34	6410	Assistance Program	1,000	1,000	$0	0.0%	
35	6415	Church Assistance Program	1,000	1,000	$0	0.0%	
36	6420	Encouragement Ministry	1,000	1,000	$0	0.0%	
37	6425	Marriage Support	1,000	1,000	$0	0.0%	
38	6430	Marriage Support / Counseling	1,000	1,000	$0	0.0%	
39	6440	Prayer Ministry	1,000	1,000	$0	0.0%	
40	6450	Stephen Ministry	1,000	1,000	$0	0.0%	
41	6460	Training	1,000	1,000	$0	0.0%	
42		**Total Pastoral Care**	**8,000**	**8,000**	**$0**	**0.0%**	1.1% / 1.1%
43							
44		**Youth Ministries**					
45	7510	Cadets	1,000	1,000	$0	0.0%	
46	7515	Children in Worship	1,000	1,000	$0	0.0%	
47	7520	Church Education - Middle & High School	1,000	1,000	$0	0.0%	
48	7525	GEMS	1,000	1,000	$0	0.0%	
49	7530	GEMS - Jr.	1,000	1,000	$0	0.0%	
50	7535	Instructional Materials - Leadership	1,000	1,000	$0	0.0%	
51	7540	Kingdom Kids	1,000	1,000	$0	0.0%	
52	7545	Little Lambs	1,000	1,000	$0	0.0%	
53	7550	Member Training	1,000	1,000	$0	0.0%	
54	7555	Middle School	1,000	1,000	$0	0.0%	
55	7560	Nurseries	1,000	1,000	$0	0.0%	
56	7565	Profession of Faith / Mentoring	1,000	1,000	$0	0.0%	
57	7575	Senior High	1,000	1,000	$0	0.0%	
58	7575	Special Events	1,000	1,000	$0	0.0%	
59	7580	Treasure Zone	1,000	1,000	$0	0.0%	
60	7585	Vacation Bible School	1,000	1,000	$0	0.0%	
61		**Total Youth Ministries**	**16,000**	**16,000**	**$0**	**0.0%**	2.3% / 2.3%
62							

PURPOSE CHURCH BUDGET SPREEDSHEET (PAGE 3.)

No.	Code	Adult Education						
63		Adult Education						
64	7010	College Ministry	1,000	1,000	$0	0.0%		
65	7015	Curriculum, speakers, materials	1,000	1,000	$0	0.0%		
66	7020	Library	1,000	1,000	$0	0.0%		
67	7025	Member Training	1,000	1,000	$0	0.0%		
68	7030	Other Adult Ministry	1,000	1,000	$0	0.0%		
69	7035	Profession of Faith/Mentoring	1,000	1,000	$0	0.0%		
70	7040	Singles Ministry	1,000	1,000	$0	0.0%		
71	7045	Small Group Ministry	1,000	1,000	$0	0.0%		
72	7050	Social Justice	1,000	1,000	$0	0.0%		
73	7055	Spiritual Gift Assessment	1,000	1,000	$0	0.0%		
74	7060	Spiritual Gift Awareness	1,000	1,000	$0	0.0%		
75	7065	Stewardship	1,000	1,000	$0	0.0%		
76		Total Adult Education	12,000	12,000	$0	0.0%	1.7%	1.7%
77								
78		Congregational Life						
79	6210	Church Anniversary	1,000	1,000	$0	0.0%		
80	6215	Church Picnic	1,000	1,000	$0	0.0%		
81	6220	Fellowship Dinners	1,000	1,000	$0	0.0%		
82	6225	Fellowship Supplies	1,000	1,000	$0	0.0%		
83	6230	Miscellaneous	1,000	1,000	$0	0.0%		
84	6240	Small Group Ministry	1,000	1,000	$0	0.0%		
85	6250	Special Events	1,000	1,000	$0	0.0%		
86	6260	Guest/New Member Enfolding	1,000	1,000	$0	0.0%		
87		Total Congregational Life	8,000	8,000	$0	0.0%	1.1%	1.1%
88								
89		Evangelism						
90	8010	Coffee Break/Story Hour	1,000	1,000	$0	0.0%		
91	8015	Community Seek and Serve Projects	1,000	1,000	$0	0.0%		
92	8020	Evang Team/Basic Discipleship (Alpha)	1,000	1,000	$0	0.0%		
93	8025	Invitational materials	1,000	1,000	$0	0.0%		
94	8030	Member Training	1,000	1,000	$0	0.0%		
95	8035	Missions Promotion and Development	1,000	1,000	$0	0.0%		

PURPOSE CHURCH BUDGET SPREEDSHEET (PAGE 4.)

#	Code	Description						
96	8040	Nativity Program	1,000		$0	0.0%		
97	8045	New Move In Ministry	1,000		$0	0.0%		
98	8050	Other Outreach Events/Seminars	1,000		$0	0.0%		
99	8055	Outreach / Advertising	1,000		$0	0.0%		
100	8060	Outreach Events	1,000		$0	0.0%		
101	8065	VBS Promotion and Followup	1,000		$0	0.0%		
102	8070	Welcome/Hospitality Ministry	1,000		$0	0.0%		
103		**Total Evangelism**	**13,000**	**13,000**	**$0**	**0.0%**	1.9%	1.8%
104								
105		**Denominational Ministry**						
106	8810	**Denominational Ministry Shares**	166,122	152,143	$13,979	9.2%		
107		> Note: 2005 = $302.04 x 550 members						
108		> Note: 2004 = $298.32 x 510 members						
109		Back to God Hour, CRC TV, Calvin College						
110		Calvin Seminary, CRC Publications						
111		Denominational Services: Fund for Smaller Churches, Home Missions,						
112		Pastoral Ministries, World						
113		Missions						
114	8820	**Classical Ministry Shares**	19,872	18,192	$1,680	9.2%		
115		> Note: 2005 = $36.13 x 550 members						
116		> Note: 2004 = $35.67 x 510 members						
117		**Total Denominational Ministry**	**185,994**	**170,335**	**$15,659**	**9.2%**	26.6%	26.4%
118								
119		**Facilities and Equipment**						
120	5510	Equipment Repairs	1,000	1,000	$0	0.0%		
121	5515	Equipment Small (<$1,000)	1,000	1,000	$0	0.0%		
122	5520	Facility Repair	1,000	1,000	$0	0.0%		

PURPOSE CHURCH BUDGET SPREEDSHEET (PAGE 5.)

#	Code	Description						
123	5525	Gardening	1,000	1,000	$0	0.0%	0.0%	
124	5530	Insurance	1,000	1,000	$0	0.0%	0.0%	
125	5540	Lawnmowing & Snowplowing	1,000	1,000	$0	0.0%	0.0%	
126	5550	Maintenance	1,000	1,000	$0	0.0%	0.0%	
127	5560	Parking Lot Repairs	1,000	1,000	$0	0.0%	0.0%	
128	5570	Utilities - Electric	1,000	1,000	$0	0.0%	0.0%	
129	5575	Utilities - Gas	1,000	1,000	$0	0.0%	0.0%	
130	5579	Utilities - Other	1,000	1,000	$0	0.0%	0.0%	
131		Total Facilities and Equipment	11,000	11,000	$0	0.0%	1.6%	1.6%
132								
133		Administration/Leadership						
134	5110	Accounting/Payroll Services	1,000	1,000	$0	0.0%	0.0%	
135	5115	Communications - Telephone, Internet	1,000	1,000	$0	0.0%	0.0%	
136	5120	Computer Updating/Maintenance	1,000	1,000	$0	0.0%	0.0%	
137	5125	Council Expense	1,000	1,000	$0	0.0%	0.0%	
138	5130	Dues & Subscriptions	1,000	1,000	$0	0.0%	0.0%	
139	5140	Dues & Subscriptions - Webhosting	1,000	1,000	$0	0.0%	0.0%	
140	5150	Legal & Professional	1,000	1,000	$0	0.0%	0.0%	
141	5160	Liability Insurance	1,000	1,000	$0	0.0%	0.0%	
142	5170	Office Equipment - Purchases and Rental	1,000	1,000	$0	0.0%	0.0%	
143	5175	Office Supplies, Paper, Postage	1,000	1,000	$0	0.0%	0.0%	
144	5176	Rent - Admin & Facilities	1,000	1,000	$0	0.0%	0.0%	
145	5180	Repairs / Improvements	1,000	1,000	$0	0.0%	0.0%	
146	5185	Taxes, Licenses & Fees	1,000	1,000	$0	0.0%	0.0%	
147	5190	Utilities	1,000	1,000	$0	0.0%	0.0%	
148	5195	Miscellaneous Expenses	1,000	1,000	$0	0.0%	0.0%	
149		Total Administration	15,000	15,000	$0	0.0%	2.1%	2.1%
150								
151		Christian Ed. Assistance (5%)	1,000	1,000	$0	0.0%	0.1%	0.1%
152								
153		Total General Fund Requests	$698,438	661,685	$36,753	5.6%	100.0%	99.3%

SAMPLE (WAGE AND BENEFITS ACCOUNTING SPREADSHEET)

Our Church

2005 Proposed Budget

Wage and Benefit Detail

	Hours per wk	Hourly Rate	Computed Wages	FICA / SECA	Health In	MPF	403b	Auto Reimb	Cont. Educ.	Wkrs' Comp.	Sabb. Fund	Total Bene.	Total Wage+Bene
Senior Pastor Salaries													
Senior Pastor	40.0	$28.85	$60,000	$3,900	$11,932	$5,288	$0	$1,500	$3,000	$0	$1,000	$26,620	$86,620
Pastor 2	40.0	$19.23	$40,000	$2,600	$11,932	$5,288	$0	$1,500	$3,000	$0	$1,000	$25,320	$65,320
Totals: FTEs / $	2.0		$100,000	$6,500	$23,864	$10,576	$0	$3,000	$6,000	$0	$2,000	$51,940	$151,940
Ministry Staff Wages													
Pastoral Care	20.0	$15.00	$15,600	$1,014	$0	$0	$0	$1,800	$0	$924	$0	$3,738	$19,338
Director of Evangelism	20.0	$15.00	$15,600	$1,193	$0	$0	$0	$0	$500	$0	$0	$1,693	$17,293
Children/Youth Ministries Coordinator	40.0	$15.00	$31,200	$2,387	$6,079	$0	$1,000	$0	$500	$0	$0	$9,966	$41,166
Seminary Intern	15.0	$15.00	$11,700	$895	$0	$0	$0	$0	$0	$0	$0	$895	$12,595
Adult Education Coordinator	40.0	$15.00	$31,200	$2,387	$3,190	$0	$1,000	$0	$500	$0	$0	$7,077	$38,277
Worship/Music Coordinator	20.0	$15.00	$15,600	$1,193	$0	$0	$0	$0	$500	$0	$0	$1,693	$17,293
Ministry Assistant	20.0	$15.00	$15,600	$1,193	$3,040	$0	$0	$0	$500	$0	$0	$4,733	$20,333
Merit allocations			$1,500	$115	$0	$0	$0	$0	$0	$0	$0	$115	$1,615
Totals: FTEs / $	4.4		$138,000	$10,377	$12,309	$0	$2,000	$1,800	$2,500	$924	$0	$29,910	$167,910
Support Staff Wages													
Church Administrator	20.0	$15.00	$15,600	$1,193	$0	$0	$0	$0	$500	$277	$0	$1,970	$17,570
Bookkeeper	6.0	$15.00	$4,680	$358	$0	$0	$0	$0	$0	$0	$0	$358	$5,038
Bulletin Secretary	10.0	$15.00	$7,800	$597	$0	$0	$0	$0	$0	$0	$0	$597	$8,397
Ministry Assistant	20.0	$15.00	$15,600	$1,193	$3,039	$0	$500	$0	$0	$0	$0	$4,732	$20,332
Secretary vacation coverage	0.0	$0.00	$0	$0	$0	$0	$0	$0	$0	$0	$0	$0	$0
Network Administrator	8.0	$15.00	$6,240	$477	$0	$0	$0	$0	$0	$0	$0	$477	$6,717
Custodian (includes overtime)	40.0	$15.00	$31,200	$2,387	$3,190	$0	$500	$0	$0	$1,109	$0	$7,186	$38,386
Custodial Asst.			$1,000	$77	$0	$0	$0	$0	$0	$0	$0	$77	$1,077
Merit allocations			$1,000	$77	$0	$0	$0	$0	$0	$0	$0	$77	$1,077
Totals: FTEs / $	2.6		$83,120	$6,359	$6,229	$0	$1,000	$0	$500	$1,386	$0	$15,474	$98,594
Grand Totals: FTEs / $	9.0		$321,120	$23,236	$42,402	$10,576	$3,000	$4,800	$9,000	$2,310	$2,000	$97,324	$418,444

ALL DEBT SUMMARY (SAMPLE)

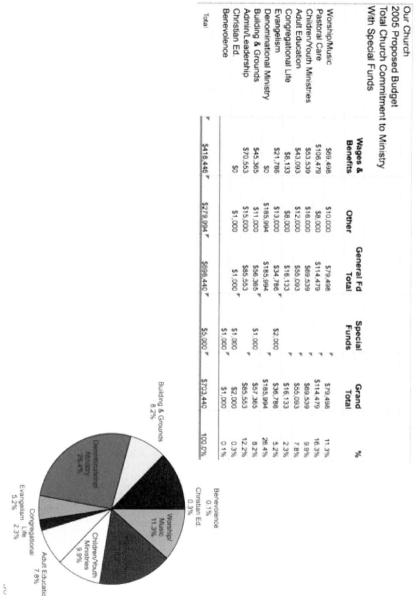

SAMPLE ALL DEBT SUMMARY

Our Church
2005 Proposed Budget
Total Church Commitment to Ministry
With Special Funds

	Wages & Benefits	Other	General Fd Total	Special Funds	Grand Total	%
Worship/Music	$69,498	$10,000	$79,498		$79,498	11.3%
Pastoral Care	$106,479	$8,000	$114,479		$114,479	16.3%
Children/Youth Ministries	$53,539	$16,000	$69,539		$69,539	9.9%
Adult Education	$43,093	$12,000	$55,093		$55,093	7.8%
Congregational Life	$8,133	$8,000	$16,133		$16,133	2.3%
Evangelism	$21,786	$13,000	$34,786	$2,000	$36,786	5.2%
Denominational Ministry	$0	$185,994	$185,994		$185,994	26.4%
Building & Grounds	$45,365	$11,000	$56,365	$1,000	$57,365	8.2%
Admin/Leadership	$70,553	$15,000	$85,553		$85,553	12.2%
Christian Ed.	$0	$1,000	$1,000	$1,000	$2,000	0.3%
Benevolence				$1,000	$1,000	0.1%
Total	$418,446	$279,994	$698,440	$5,000	$703,440	100.0%

Building & Grounds 8.2%
Denominational Ministry 26.4%
Evangelism 5.2%
Congregational Life 2.3%
Adult Education 7.8%
Children/Youth Ministries 9.9%
Worship/Music 11.3%
Christian Ed. 0.3%
Benevolence 0.1%

SAMPLE
FORMS
AND
TEMPLATES

Personal
Budget Planner

TABLE ONE	Current Spending	Necessary Changes	Planned Budget
Essential Monthly Expenses	$	$	$
HOME			
Rent or Mortgage			
Electricity			
Water/Sewer/Garbage			
Telephone - Land line			
Telephone - Mobile			
FOOD			
Groceries			
School Lunches			
Work Lunches			
Other			
TRANSPORTATION			
Car Payment			
Car Insurance			
Gasoline			
Repairs & Maintenance			
Public Transportation			
OTHER BASIC EXPENSES			
Child Care			
Child Support			
Clothing			
Haircuts / Personal Care			
Insurance: Life, Health, Disability, etc.			
Laundry, Dry Cleaning			
Medical & Dental			
Prescriptions			
Newspaper			
Cable TV			
School Expenses			
Taxes: IRS, Property			
SAVINGS			
Emergencies			
Long-Term Goals			
Retirement			
Short-Term Goals			
Total Essential Monthy Expenses	$	$	$

TABLE TWO	Current Spending	Necessary Changes	Planned Budget
Other Monthly Expenses	$	$	$
CREDIT CARD PAYMENTS			
INSTALLMENT LOAN PAYMENTS			
ENTERTAINMENT			
Eating Out or Ordering In			
Movie Tickets			
Plays / Concerts			
Movie Rentals			
CD's, Music downloads			
Sporting Events			
Internet Access Fees			
Books, Magazines, Newspapers			
Other			
Other			
CLUBS/ORGANIZATIONS			
Gym / Health Club Dues			
Association Dues / Expenses			
Professional Organization Dues			
Social Organization Dues			
Other			
GIFTS			
Gifts & Cards (holidays, birthdays, etc.)			
Religious Tithes			
Charitable Contributions			
PETS			
Veterinary Expenses			
Pet Food			
MISCELLANEOUS EXPENSES			
Children's Allowances			
Vacations			
Occupational License Fees			
Cigarettes / Tobacco			
Alcoholic Beverages			
Snacks			
Other			
Total Other Expense			
Total Essential Monthly Expenses			
Total Living Expenses	$	$	$

MONTHLY INCOME	Gross Income	Net Income
Income 1		
Income 2		
Other Income (child support, social security, military retirement, etc.)		
TOTAL GROSS/NET INCOME	$	$

(Total Net Monthly Income) - (Total Monthly Living Expenses) = (+ or -)

$_____ - _____ = _____

Commitment That Lasts Generations

B-1

[CHURCH NAME]
Church Vision and Goals Process For 2017 (Sample Process)
Use this process to complete the form below (Church Vision and Goals For 2017).

The mission of the [Church Name] is to *make disciples of Jesus Christ for the transformation of the world*, and our local churches provide the most significant place to make disciples. As a part of the [Conference Name], we all have to do our part in order to fulfill this mission by moving toward our preferred future: ***Great Leaders – Great Churches – Great Disciples – Transformed World***.

The annual [Conference Name] is an opportunity to evaluate and celebrate who your congregation is aligning your vision and goals to answer God's call to greatness.

The process outlined below is designed to be used by the Church Council (or other appropriate group) as you develop your ministry for the coming year. ***Prayer is essential to this process!***

Note: *Some congregations use a different process or timeframe to do the vision and goal setting – You don't have to repeat the process. Record your information on the form as best as you can or provide another format.*

I.   Clarify Your Vision

Think of your vision as your motto: *A short phrase (10 words or less) that's easy to remember, expressing the beliefs or ideals which guide your congregation to make disciples of Jesus Christ for the transformation of the world.* An effective vision statement should be biblical, specific, motivating and measurable. Keep it brief! You want both the community and your congregation to remember it and understand that this is why you do what you do. Recite it in worship and at meetings; use it in prayers, in print and in public;…and most of all, live it out! The vision may remain the same from year to year.

Each congregation expresses their vision in unique ways that reflect God's call for the members, their gifts, and the needs of their particular setting. For example, the vision of a congregation in a diverse neighborhood might be, *"meeting people, meeting needs, meeting Christ."* In a rural setting, challenged by declining population and services, a congregation might experience God's call to a ministry of *"living and giving God's hope for all times."*

II.   Assess Your Current Reality

Gather information on your ministry setting and measurements of your ministry efforts. There are resources to include:

- **Vital Signs** – Each local church is asked to submit weekly statistics through the dashboard on the [Website Name]. If your congregation is doing so, you may access the requested numbers through the executive summary on the following site: [Website URL].

If your congregation used the vision/goal-setting process for the current year, evaluate your progress by answering the following questions:

1. How are you getting the congregation and community familiarized with your vision?
2. Which goals and strategies have worked and will be beneficial to continue?
3. What challenges and/or roadblocks have you encountered, and how do you plan to move past them?

4. What "glory sightings" and stories will you tell your congregation – when did you see God at work, deepening your discipleship and bringing transformation to others' lives through your members and your ministries?

III.   Identify 2-3 Attainable Goals for 2017 that are Aligned with Your Vision

Way too often we make a long list of things we're going to do as a congregation and call those "Goals" but they're not. Goals are the answer to the question, "What 2-3 big ideas can we accomplish that will have the greatest impact on our ability to live out our vision?"

Example: After prayer and discussion, the diverse neighborhood congregation (mentioned above) set two goals:

1. To have at least 50% of the congregation actively involved in at least one ministry away from the church property that is *"meeting people, meeting needs, meeting Christ"*.
2. As a congregation, to become familiar with the cultures represented in the neighborhood.

Note: If a goal isn't accomplished in one year, it may be continued into the next year with updated strategies.

IV.   Plan the Year's Strategies

Think about steps that your committees and groups (Sunday School, Choir, Finance Committee…) can take to help reach those goals. List a few strategies for each goal. These strategies may continue to develop even after the [Conference Name].

Example: The [Committee Name] hosts cultural celebrations at the church. Education designates one month of Sunday School when all ages learn about the Great Commission and how to talk about Christ outside of the congregation. The Worship Committee will organize a "Christ for the World" worship service in a neighborhood park and involve the church's neighbors in its planning.

V.   Indicate Vitality Trainings in which you are Planning to Participate

Each year, various opportunities are offered by the conference, districts, and others in order to create **Great Churches, Great Leaders, and Great Disciples.**

Check out these options:

- Abide (leadership initiative for small membership churches) – [Website URL]
- [Conference Name] (Conference for small membership churches) – [Website URL]
- Next Steps (Process of training and support for congregations to continue moving toward greater vitality) – [Website URL]
- Transforming Communities ([State] Leadership Center) – [Website URL]
- Leadership Institute - – [Website URL]

For more ideas, check on the conference website (website url), the [Church Name] website (website url), or with your district office.

[CHURCH NAME]
Church Vision and Goals For 2017 (Sample Form)

Refer to your previous year's Vision and Goals Process to complete this form!
You can provide your own format for this information as long as you cover the basic categories.

Vision: _____

_____

2015	2016	Vital Signs
		Average worship attendance at all regularly-held weekly services
		Total number of people received by profession of faith
		Average number of people participating in small groups
		Average number of people serving in mission/outreach
		Total amount given for support of benevolent and charitable ministries
		Total offering received

Evaluate and Celebrate 2016 Goals: What have you accomplished in this year so far? What still needs to be done? List the goals and describe their status, adding more as needed.

Goal #1:

Goal #2:

Goal #3:

Set 2017 Goals and Strategies: What are your plans to do in the coming year? How do you plan on accomplishing it? List goals with the steps for making them happen, adding more as needed. **Note:** *Goals may be continued from the current year to the next year if they're not yet complete.*

Goal #1:
•
•
•
•
Goal #2:
•
•
•
•
Goal #3:
•
•
•
•

Receive Vitality Training – Check/List those in which you're interested or plan to participate.

☐ ABIDE

☐ Next Steps

☐ Transforming Communities in [City, State]

☐ Leadership Institute at [Church Name] in [City, State]

☐ District/Regional Event: _____

☐ Other: _____

[Church Name]
Church Officer List 20___

Please use this form to list your church officers for the 20___ church year. A maximum of 14 officers' listings can appear on each page; other officers' names will be placed on various mailing lists for use by Conference Departmental personnel. **Please note that officer listings shown with asterisk (*) are required information.** If you area codes/phone prefixes have changed, please be sure to list them. If directions to the church have changed, please update them at the end of this form. Please **TYPE OR PRINT ONLY** names, addresses and zip codes and check for accuracy. Email your completed report to ___ _____ or mail your list to _____ _____ to arrive by _____, _____. **Faxed reports can be accepted if they are typed or printed. Fax to _____.** Thank you for your prompt help.

Church Name:		Phone#:	
Street Address:		Fax#:	
City, State & Zip:		Email:	Website:
Attn: Mail Address:			
(Use P.O. Box if valid: Large packages cannot be sent to post office box.)			
Bulk Mail Address:			
(Use street address only: Bulk mail cannot be sent to post office box.)			
Sunday School beings at:	Worship Service begins:	Bilingual Services:	We have regular mid-week
meetings on this day:	At this time:	Church Secretary:	Email:

Position	Name	Address	Phone#	Email
Pastor*			Home: Cell:	
Associate* Pastor(s)			Home: Cell:	
First* Elder			Home: Cell:	
Head Deacon			Home: Cell:	
Clerk*			Home: Cell:	
Treasurer*			Home: Cell:	
Children's* Ministries			Home: Cell:	
Community* Services Dir.			Home: Cell:	
Education Secretary			Home: Cell:	
Health* Ministries			Home: Cell:	
Men's* Ministries			Home: Cell:	
Women's* Ministries			Home: Cell:	
Prayer* Ministries			Home: Cell:	
Communication* Leader			Home: Cell:	

[Church Name] **Church Officer List 20___ (Page 2)**				
Religious* Liberty			Home: Cell:	
Risk Managemt.*			Home: Cell:	
Sunday* School Supt.			Home: Cell:	
Stewardship Leader			Home: Cell:	
Youth* Leader			Home: Cell:	
Pathfinder* Leader			Home: Cell:	
Adventurer* Leader			Home: Cell:	
Personal Min* Leader			Home: Cell:	
Reconnecting* Ministries Coordinator			Home: Cell:	
			Home: Cell:	
			Home: Cell:	
			Home: Cell:	
			Home: Cell:	
			Home: Cell:	
			Home: Cell:	
			Home: Cell:	
			Home: Cell:	
			Home: Cell:	
			Home: Cell:	
			Home: Cell:	
			Home: Cell:	

Please update directions to your church:

Please <u>double check</u> the directions to your church and make the necessary corrections! The directions should begin from the Conference office to your church.

Name of Person Filling Out this Form:

Phone Number:

Church Member Survey

1. Gender:
- o Male
- o Female

2. Race or ethnicity:
- o Anglo/White
- o Asian
- o Black/African American
- o Hispanic
- o Other

3. Age group:
- o Under 18
- o 18-24
- o 25-34
- o 35-44
- o 44-54
- o 55-64
- o 65+

4. Current marital status:
- o Never married
- o Married
- o Widowed
- o Divorced/separated

5. Highest educational status you have achieved (for ages 25 and up):

- o Grade 0-8
- o Some high school, grade 9-11
- o High school graduate
- o Some college, 1-3 years
- o Associate degree
- o Bachelor's degree
- o Post-graduate studies/degree

6. Residence:
- o Own (or buying)
- o Rent (or leasing)

7. Type of housing:
- o Single family house
- o Duplex
- o Apartment/condo/townhouse
- o Mobile home/trailer

8. How long have you lived at your current address?
- o Less than 1 year
- o 1-4 years
- o 5-14 years
- o 15 or more years

9. On average, how long does it take you to travel from your home to this church?
- o Less than 10 minutes
- o 10-20 minutes
- o 21-30 minutes
- o More than 30 minutes

10. Number of persons currently living in your home (include yourself):
- o 1
- o 2
- o 3
- o 4
- o 5+

11. Indicate the range of your total annual family income:
- o Less than $15,000
- o $15,000-$29,999
- o $30,000-$49,999
- o $50,000-$74,999
- o $75,000-$99,999
- o $100,000 or more

Church Member Survey - Page 2

12. Mark the <u>one</u> category that best describes you <u>now</u>:
- o Admin. support (secretary, cashier, etc.)
- o Craftsman (foreman, mechanic, etc.)
- o Manager (administrator, self-employed)
- o Sales (underwriter, sales worker, etc.)
- o Professional (doctor, teacher, etc.)
- o Service (police, health worker, etc.)
- o Laborer (construction, stockman, etc.)
- o Farming, fishing, forestry
- o Homemaker
- o Student (full-time)
- o Unemployed
- o Retired

13. How long have you been a Christian?
- o Not a Christian
- o Less than 1 year
- o 1-5 years
- o 6-10 years
- o More than 10 years

14. How long have you been a member of this church?
- o Not a member
- o Less than 1 year
- o 1-5 years
- o 6-10 years
- o More than 10 years

15. How did you first hear about this church? Mark only one:
- o Advertisement or sign
- o Radio or TV program
- o Internet
- o I found it on my own
- o I was invited by a friend, relative, or church member

16. Mark up to <u>three</u> of the following that influenced you to join/attend this church:
- o It's a friendly church
- o It's located near my home
- o Liked the activities of the church
- o Liked the facilities
- o Liked the pastor and/or staff
- o Liked the Sunday School/small group
- o Personal visit by church member or staff
- o Activities offered for my children
- o Common interests with members
- o Liked the worship style
- o This was/is my family's church

17. How would you rate each of the following in your church? (1=excellent, 2=good, 3=fair, 4=not offered or don't know)

	1	2	3	4
Sunday AM Worship	o	o	o	o
Sunday PM Worship	o	o	o	o
Sunday School	o	o	o	o
Mid-Week Prayer Service	o	o	o	o
Children/Preschool Ministry	o	o	o	o
Women's Ministry	o	o	o	o
Men's Ministry	o	o	o	o
Discipleship	o	o	o	o
Youth Ministry	o	o	o	o
Music Ministry	o	o	o	o
Stewardship Program	o	o	o	o
Outreach/Visitation	o	o	o	o

STRATEGY PLANNING
NEW MEMBER QUESTIONNAIRE

1. How did you join this church? (Please check one)
_____ First-time decision/baptism
_____ Statement
_____ Transfer of letter

2. How long have you been a member?
_____ Months
_____ Years

3. How far do you live from the church? (Please answer one)
_____ Miles, or
_____ Minutes in drive time

4. Generally, in what direction do you travel home from the church?
___ North   ___ South   ___ East   ___ West
or from the city/town of _____

5. Did you have any family members (immediate or extended) active in this church before you joined? If yes, describe them (parent, sister, aunt, etc.).

Name   Relationship
_____   _____
_____   _____
_____   _____

6. What activity did you first come to when visiting our church?
_____

7. What other activity, if any, did you attend on your first visit?
_____

8. What did you see or experience during your first visits to the church that made you want to return?

_____

_____

_____

9. Did you have a contact/visit/invitation from someone at this church that led you to visit on that fist occasion? If yes, describe who contacted you and how? _____ Yes _____ No

_____

_____

10. Did you have a contact/visit/invitation from someone at this church <u>after</u> your first visit that led you to return a second time? If yes, describe who contacted you and how. _____ Yes _____ No

_____

_____

11. For you and/or your family, what is the most important ministry/program of this church (or perhaps the one that led you to join the church)?

_____

_____

12. On a scale of one to ten, describe your satisfaction level about this church (put an "x" at the appropriate spot):

1 - **5** - **10**
Not Satisfied   Very Satisfied

What suggestions do you have for enhancing the worship/ministry experience at this church?

_____

_____

_____

_____

_____

Time, Talent and Giftedness Survey

Name: _____ Date: _____

Address: _____ City: _____ Zip: _____

Email: _____ Phone: _____

Place an "x" in the box beside the ministry area in which you would like to serve. All information on these sheets will remain confidential among church staff/leadership.

1. I am interested in serving in the following areas when the church body meets:

[   ] Preschool (ages birth to 4 years) **
[   ] Children (grades K through 5th) **
[   ] Middle school (grades 6 through 8) **
[   ] High school (grades 9 through 12) **
[   ] College and Career (ages 18-29)
[   ] Adults
[   ] Senior adults
[   ] Divorced
[   ] Married couples
[   ] Blended families
[   ] Single parents
[   ] Singles
[   ] Widows
[   ] Audio / visual
[   ] Backyard Bible clubs
[   ] Baptism
[   ] Drama

[   ] Fellowship / Hospitality / Refreshments
[   ] Greeter
[   ] Hospital visitation
[   ] Missions volunteer
[   ] Music (instrument) _____
[   ] Music (vocal)
[   ] Neighborhood Bible study
[   ] Outreach
[   ] Prayer
[   ] Publicity (posters, signs, flyers)
[   ] Setup (chairs & tables)
[   ] Special event planning
[   ] Teardown (chairs & tables)
[   ] Usher / offerings
[   ] Web / Internet
[   ] Writing cards/notes
[   ] Other: _____

*** Please note that for liability reasons, anyone working with children or youth will be required to have a criminal background check. There are no exceptions.*

2. I have a passion for and experience in the following area(s):

[   ] Baking
[   ] Building things
[   ] Counting (numbers, money)
[   ] Creating objects of beauty
[   ] Decorating
[   ] Encouraging others
[   ] Evaluating and analyzing data
[   ] Giving financially
[   ] Leading or facilitating teams
[   ] Listening to others
[   ] Making others welcome
[   ] Making phone calls
[   ] Mentoring
[   ] Managing others

[   ] PC hardware/software
[   ] Planning and directing work
[   ] Providing compassionate care
[   ] Providing meals for sick members
[   ] Providing truck or towing service
[   ] Recruiting others
[   ] Relating to other cultures
[   ] Research
[   ] Sharing the Gospel with others
[   ] Storytelling
[   ] Substitute teaching
[   ] Wedding planning/hostess
[   ] Writing articles, letters, books
[   ] Other: _____

Name: _____ Date: _____

3. I can serve the church and community through personal skills and talents in:

Construction/Repair
[　] AC/Furnace repair
[　] Cabinetry
[　] Carpentry
[　] Carpet and tile
[　] Electrical
[　] Flooring
[　] Furniture repair
[　] Heavy lifting
[　] Landscaping / lawn care
[　] Mechanics
[　] Painting
[　] Plumbing
[　] Roofing
[　] Sheetrock
[　] Other: _____

Arts
[　] Acting
[　] Artwork
[　] Calligraphy
[　] Clowning
[　] Computer graphics
[　] Costumes
[　] Crafts
[　] Dance
[　] Drawing
[　] Floral arrangements
[　] Photography/video
[　] Puppetry
[　] Sewing / Quilting
[　] Staging/Props
[　] Other: _____

Education
[　] English as 2nd Language
[　] Foreign language
[　] Mathematics
[　] Reading
[　] Teaching / tutoring

Miscellaneous
[　] Accounting
[　] Childcare
[　] Driving/transportation
[　] General housekeeping
[　] Insurance
[　] Meal preparation
[　] Real Estate
[　] Other: _____

4. I would like to serve the community and individuals in the area(s) of:

[　] Adoption / foster care
[　] AIDS
[　] Alcohol addiction
[　] Blindness
[　] Blood drives
[　] Clothes pantry
[　] Crisis pregnancy
[　] Deaf ministry
[　] Diet and nutrition
[　] Disaster relief

[　] Ethnic/cultural diversity
[　] Food pantry
[　] Grief care
[　] Habitat for Humanity
[　] Homebound care
[　] Homelessness
[　] Homosexuality
[　] Literacy
[　] Loneliness
[　] Multi-housing

[　] Mental health issues
[　] Narcotic addictions
[　] Nursing home ministry
[　] Physical abuse
[　] Physical handicaps
[　] Physical health issues
[　] Pornography addictions
[　] Prison ministry
[　] World hunger
[　] Other: _____

5. I am interested helping with the following area(s) of sports and recreation:

[　] Baseball / softball
[　] Basketball
[　] Biking
[　] Bowling
[　] Camping
[　] Exercise
[　] Fishing

[　] Football
[　] Golf
[　] Hiking
[　] Ice-skating / hockey
[　] Rock climbing
[　] Roller blading / skating
[　] Running / jogging

[　] Skateboarding
[　] Snow skiing
[　] Soccer
[　] Swimming
[　] Tennis
[　] Volleyball
[　] Other: _____

6. I am available at the following time(s):

[　] Mornings
[　] Afternoons
[　] Evenings

[　] Weekdays
[　] Weekends
[　] Weekends

[　] As Needed

[　] One-time projects
[　] Short-term projects

[　] At home projects
[　] Long-term projects

Name: _____   Date: _____

7. What occupational or professional experience(s) do you have that might help others?

_____

_____

_____

8. What educational experience(s) do you have that might help others?

_____

_____

_____

9. What personal or life experiences do you have that you can use in ministry?

_____

_____

_____

10. What painful experiences or trials could you relate to and encourage others going through similar experiences?

_____

_____

_____

11. Describe spiritual experiences that have been meaningful to you?

_____

_____

_____

12. In which volunteer organizations have you served, and in what capacity?

_____

_____

_____

Name: _____ Date: _____

13. In what area(s) are you spiritually gifted by God?

[   ] I don't know or am not completely certain. I want to know more about spiritual gifts.

[   ] **Administration**: I am a goal and object-oriented individual who has strong organizational abilities. It is possible for me to coordinate resources in order to accomplish tasks as quickly as possible.

[   ] **Evangelism**: I am one with a strong desire to share the Gospel with unbelievers in every possible situation and through all possible means.

[   ] **Exhortation**: I have a special ability to encourage others in the body of Christ by giving them words of comfort, courage and counsel at times of need or crisis.

[   ] **Giving**: I have the ability to give material goods and financial resources with joy, so that the needs of the Lord's work are met.

[   ] **Helps**: I am one who is motivated by the desire to further the ministry by meeting genuine needs of another individual. I am usually helping someone in a leadership position.

[   ] **Hospitality**: I have the ability to make guests feel comfortable and "at home."

[   ] **Leadership**: I have the ability to lead others toward spiritual growth; a visionary with the ability to set goals and motivate others toward accomplishing these goals.

[   ] **Mercy**: I am one who has immediate compassion for those suffering physically, mentally or emotionally. I derive great joy in meeting the needs of others.

[   ] **Prophecy**: I have the ability to proclaim God's truth without compromise. I have strong convictions and am persuasive in defining right and wrong.

[   ] **Service**: I have the ability to perform any task with joy that benefits others and meets practical needs.

[   ] **Shepherding**: I have the unique ability to take responsibility for the long-term spiritual growth of a group of believers. I assume responsibility to guide, feed and protect the flock.

[   ] **Teaching**: I have the ability to research and explain God's truth so there is understanding and application in the lives of others.

14. What else would you like to share with the church staff?

_____

_____

_____

_____

_____

Discovering Your Spiritual Gifts

Instructions

This worksheet is designed to assist you in identifying your strengths as specifically related to ministry and service in the local church. Its primary purpose is to enable you to identify areas of ministry for which you are most likely gifted. It is not designed to be an exhaustive analysis of spiritual gifts, but rather to highlight areas of strength based on what you feel motivates you spiritually.

You will fill in a "score" on the worksheet in the box corresponding to the statement number based on the following scoring system:

Score	How This Statement Best Describes Me
0	I am seldom or never this way
1	I am usually not this way
2	I am this way some of the time
3	I am this way most or all of the time

Keep in mind when you score yourself that most of these are desirable traits for a Christian to have, and giving yourself a 0 or a 1 on a particular trait does not mean that you are unspiritual, but rather that it is not a primary motivating factor for you as an individual.

Add up your scores for each column at the bottom of the worksheet pages. Transfer these totals to the Gifts Analysis page for each associated column. Take note in particular of the columns having the higher scores. These are probably representative of areas in which you are most gifted or motivated.

The contents of this worksheet are for your information only. Therefore, be honest and open in evaluating yourself. Remember that while we should all have good qualities as Christians, there are differences in motives and in how we express the unique character that each of us has been gifted with by God.

As a member of the body of Christ, you are very crucial to the overall health and strength of the body. We will only function as effectively as God intends if each member is doing its part. That is why we have a strong conviction that each member have a place in active ministry, and we hope that this worksheet will be helpful in finding that place of service that God intends for you.

Spiritual Gifts Worksheet – Page 1
Place Scores in the Shaded Box Next to the Statement

	A	B	C	D	E	F
1. I like to organize and plan.	▨					
2. I want to spend time with unbelievers so I can share my faith.		▨				
3. I enjoy being asked to share advice or being an encouragement to others.			▨			
4. It is important to me that the money I give to the church is used as effectively as possible.				▨		
5. I am more strongly motivated by the idea of meeting a need than performing the task.					▨	
6. I prefer to be led by others.					▨	
7. I enjoy setting goals and then making plans to meet those goals.	▨					
8. I rapidly meet the needs of others for help.					▨	
9. I have the ability to make strangers feel at ease.						▨
10. Teaching that can't be applied bothers me.			▨			
11. I thrive on organizing people, ideas and resources to improve efficiency.	▨					
12. I have an overwhelming desire to share the gospel with unbelievers.		▨				
13. I like assisting others in resolving difficult questions in their lives.			▨			
14. I notice when others have a material or financial need.				▨		
15. I like having people visit my home.						▨
16. I enjoy meeting non-Christians, even total strangers.		▨				
17. I trust that God will meet all of my needs so that I can give sacrificially a portion of all my income.				▨		
18. I enjoy welcoming guests and making them feel comfortable.						▨
Add Scores in Each Column and Log Here →						
	A	**B**	**C**	**D**	**E**	**F**

Spiritual Gifts Worksheet – Page 2

Place Scores in the Shaded Box Next to the Statement

	G	H	I	J	K	L
19. Those who are in distress seem drawn to me.		▒				
20. I have a burden to disciple others so that they can help one another.					▒	
21. Often, groups in which I am involved look to me to lead them.	▒					
22. I am compelled to unmask sin in other people.			▒			
23. I have the ability to make difficult passages of scripture understandable.						▒
24. I have the ability to make decisions rapidly and stand by them.	▒					
25. I enjoy being used by God to teach and caution large groups of believers.			▒			
26. I like projects that require a hands-on approach.				▒		
27. I care more about relationships than tasks.					▒	
28. I enjoy spending a lot of time studying the Bible so I can share these truths with others.						▒
29. I like doing special things for people who are sick or having difficulties.		▒				
30. I consider myself a task-oriented person.				▒		
31. I find contentment studying God's Word and communicating my understanding with others.						▒
32. I have the ability of helping groups of all sizes in making decisions.	▒					
33. I am greatly concerned with being a comfort to others.		▒				
34. I want my instruction to cause others to see what God is saying and to respond.			▒			
35. I prefer following rather than leading.					▒	
36. I desire to care for the spiritual well-being of a group of Christians over an extended time.					▒	
Add Scores in Each Column and Log Here →						
	G	**H**	**I**	**J**	**K**	**L**

Gifts Analysis

Compute totals by adding columns down from the previous pages and writing total scores in the boxes below. For example, the total for questions 1, 7 and 11 would be written in box "A" below.

A	B	C	D	E	F	G	H	I	J	K	L

A. _____ Administration
B. _____ Evangelism
C. _____ Exhortation
D. _____ Giving
E. _____ Helps
F. _____ Hospitality
G. _____ Leadership
H. _____ Mercy
I. _____ Prophecy
J. _____ Service
K. _____ Shepherding
L. _____ Teaching

Below is a summary of each of the qualities that are identified by this worksheet. Along with giving you insight into your own motivations, these should be helpful in directing you toward areas of service that will utilize the strengths God has given you.

Summary of Spiritual Gifts

Administration: A goal and object-oriented individual who has strong organizational abilities that make it possible to coordinate resources in order to accomplish tasks as quickly as possible.

Evangelism: One with a strong desire to share the Gospel with unbelievers in every possible situation and through all possible means.

Exhortation: A special ability to encourage others in the body of Christ by giving them words of comfort, courage and counsel at times of need or crisis.

Giving: The ability to give material goods and financial resources with joy, so that the needs of the Lord's work are met.

Helps: One who is motivated by the desire to further the ministry by meeting genuine needs of another individual, usually someone in a leadership position.

Hospitality: The ability to make guests feel comfortable and "at home."

Leadership: The ability to lead others toward spiritual growth; a visionary with the ability to set goals and motivate others toward accomplishing these goals.

Mercy: One who has immediate compassion for those suffering physically, mentally or emotionally. This person derives great joy in meeting the needs of others.

Prophecy: The ability to proclaim God's truth without compromise. This person has strong convictions and is persuasive in defining right and wrong.

Service: The ability to perform any task with joy that benefits others and meets practical needs.

Shepherding: The unique ability to take responsibility for the long-term spiritual growth of a group of believers; assumes responsibility to guide, feed and protect the flock.

Teaching: The ability to research and explain God's truth so there is understanding and application in the lives of others.

BUDGETING PROCESS

OVERVIEW

One issue that is paramount in doing a budget is getting the people to buy into the budget through ownership (*my* budget verses *their* budget). Once this occurs then they will have the confidence to realize the wisdom of the budget and the purpose of the budge. This requires a maximum number of church members to be involved in developing the annual budget. Such involvement could be construed as dangerous in that no one person has control over the final outcome, it is a product of the empowerment of the church.

A method of involving the most people in the budgeting process is most likely to produce these results. This process should produce top-down support for the budget and purpose of the church.

A group of church leaders needs to be organized as a budget committee to orchestrate the development of the budget. Typically this can be the Church Council or other body of leadership. Most important is that the leadership of the church is integrally involved in the process (fairness with no agendas except to seek out God's will). This group of people should begin their task at least five months prior to the beginning of the new fiscal year.

The charter for this group is to develop an annual church budget, which is tiled implicitly to the mission and vision and resources of the church. It should be chaired by the chairman of the finance or stewardship committee (that group which has oversight of fiscal matters of the church)). The group should include as many key leaders in the church as possible. Often these leaders can be found in positions of lay leadership as committee chairs. Don't limit the participation to just these, but include other key people, as you are aware of them.

The Finance/Stewardship Committee establish the overall budget amount for the upcoming fiscal year. This is done with foresight into potential growth in revenue and challenges in ministry. The budget should be attainable and realistic, but challenging.

Each committee and organization that requires a budget line item is given the opportunity to request funding or specific activities. The guidelines given to these requesting agencies is that each request be supportive of a goal of the church as determined in the strategic plan or the Church Council. Any request that cannot be tied rigidly to the five-fold ministry of the church (discipleship, evangelism, fellowship ministry, and worship) should be denied. All requests should reflect the vision of that committee or organization as they sense God's direction. Those specific requests should be itemized and prioritized with adequate rationale given to explain their request.

The church staff (or some identified agency) should receive each and every budget request and review them for completeness, comprehensiveness, and redundancies. Where required they should make corrections and adjustments. The refined requests should then go to the Budget Workshop.

The refined budget requests should be discussed with all budget participants having B-20 opportunity to discuss and approve each request. The requesting agency must given defense to their request and prove the case for receiving funding for specific activities. The workshop does not vote or approve budget requests until the last discussion is made. A running total of requested funding is maintained by the workshop moderator. When the total approved matches the established budget amount, the workshop participants must then shift and refine resources to maximize the effectiveness of the budget. When finally approved, the budget goes to the church for discussion and vote.

DRAFT REQUEST

This rightly begins with a visioning meeting where the committees or organizations discern where God is leading the in ministry. One way of accomplishing this is through a process of identifying (1) strengths, (2) weaknesses, (3) threats, and (4) opportunities for ministry. Members should be challenged to review the opportunities set before them for ministry, the resources God as laid at their disposal to perform ministry and discern where the church should be going.

It is important that each ministry or committee responsible for projected expenditures realize that their activities are not in a vacuum, but they must coordinate with other agencies to support one another. Thus, budget requests might well depend on the activities of other ministries. Ministry leaders should realize their need to work together in this request process.

The staff should prepare a draft calendar for the budget preparation that includes most projected church-wide activities, such as VBS, revivals, and mission trips. This is intended to remind ministries of potential impacts to their budgets and not to limit their vision.

Each organization or ministry within the church should be asked to provide a draft budget request. It is important that these requests be tied directly to the mission statement of the church. People should realize that the church is on mission and is directing its resources to the accomplishment of that mission. These requests should be solicited two months before any decision needs to be made. It would be best to use a handout for guiding the preparation of these requests. Appendix A has a suggested format.

The staff should then review the draft requests to discern obvious overlaps and redundancies. With annotations they are then forwarded to the budgeting committee.

When completed, key people of the budgeting committee or staff should review these draft requests to determine what changes need to be made, if any. This is important in that unrealistic numbers or missing information may skew the budgeting process.

Upon accomplishing this review the draft budget request is returned to the organization or ministry for consideration of changes or inclusions. A revision is expected for the upcoming budget workshop. Assigned people will take these suggested changes back to the originating groups and negotiate the necessary changes.

WORKSHOP

This is a time when the decisions of the final budget are to be made. Everyone involved in the budgeting process will have an active participation in the determination of the final budget. The workshop is designed to provide the maximum number of people the opportunity to know how the mission of the church will be tied to budget allocations and church resources.

Plan to invest 5 or 6 hours in this budget workshop. It should be scheduled at a time to provide the maximum participation; a Saturday or Sunday is preferred. The place for this meeting should be large enough to comfortably handle the number of people attending and provide resources necessary for the decision process. One necessary resource would be an overhead projector and viewing screen. It may also include a video projector for computer generated spreadsheet presentations.

Seating should be provided for the budgeting committee and all participants. In order, each participant will present his or her budget request with rationale. Both the budgeting committee and other requesting agencies will have full opportunity to understand their request and how it fits into the overall mission of the church.

As a tool to coordinate the workshop, Appendix B contains a view graph that can be used for discussion and decision-making.

It would prove beneficial to analyze the previous year budget to provide some insight for the group. If possible, each budget item should be identified by its function in the ministry of the church. Typically there are five recognized ministries of the local church: (1) evangelism or witnessing, (2) education or discipleship, (3) worship, (4) ministry and (5) fellowship. Possibly some balance should be preserved in these functions. This would necessitate that expenditures such as stamps, and salaries and utilities be designated for support of the relative function. This is not impossible, but must be intentional to be descriptive of reality. Other ways to analyze a budget may include looking at expenditures related to specific age groups: (1) adults, (2) youth and (3) children or some other breakdown. Such analysis can give insight into spending priorities.

No decisions should be made until all budget requesters have had full opportunity to make their request before the committee. If decisions are made during this time then all available resources will probably be depleted before each agency has had opportunity to make their request. A the conclusion of the budget requests the budgeting committee will begin to deliberate on the allocations for each requesting agency. Each member of the budgeting committee and each representative of the requesting agency will be given a vote in the final decision for allocating budget monies.

By the conclusion of this workshop the final budget numbers should be allocated. The final action of the workshop is that every member should be able to give vote of affirmation to support the proposed budget.

The people of God respond to the challenges set before them. Stewardship awareness and education are more than annual sermons. The people need to be challenged to consider what part they should bear in the support of the operation and conduct of the church. This provides the opportunity to set before God's people their responsibilities and also determine where they are at in their spiritual journey.

DISCUSSION

Two weeks prior to the adoption of the annual budget, designate a time for a presentation of the proposed budget before the entire congregation. A Sunday evening would suffice for this presentation. It might be optimal to do this in a morning worship service where the doctrine of stewardship is promoted.

No decisions are to be made at this meeting; it is only a time for discussion and review. The church may decide to make this meeting an approved business meeting to give the congregation assurance that they have a direct input into the final budget. In any event, information which comes out of this meeting may well lead to changes in the final budget when further consideration is given. The congregation should realize that there is still an opportunity to make changes if they deem necessary.

VOTE

The adoption of the annual budget should be made by secret ballot during a morning worship service. This vote will be taken without discussion from the floor. By this time the church congregation has had ample opportunity to review the proposed budget and amend it. It is now time for a decision. It should be stressed that stewardship is more than money, it also includes our time and abilities.

Planning Group _____

Chairman _____

MISSION TO BUDGET WORKSHOP

Pray for God's leadership as your group dreams and plans for 20____. Define the work your ministry group will contribute to the church mission statement. Then develop strategies that enable your committee/organization to join _____ Church **addressing** needs and objectives that help us fulfill our mission. YOU SHOULD **NOT** START WITH LAST YEAR'S EVENTS AND PROGRAMS AND THEN TRY TO DUPLICATE LAST YEAR.

Together we want to ask God to reveal His will and show us what He desires for us to do.

Vision Statement:

Please follow these steps:

I.   What is the purpose of your organization in light of the church's mission?

II. With your purpose in mind, what are the objectives your group will attempt this year?

   1.

   2.

   3.

   4.

III. What action plans will help you with objectives?

    1.

    2.

    3.

    4.

IV. Budget Request (By Action Plan)

    Action Plan 1 _____

    Action Plan 2 _____

    Action Plan 3 _____

Action Plan 4 _____

Action Plan 5 _____

Action Plan 6 _____

DEADLINE FOR THE RETURN OF BUDGET REQUESTS: _____

Planning Group _____ Chairperson _____

INSTRUCTIONS

I. How does your organization or ministry fit into the overall mission of the church? Develop a statement of how your organization can help to make that mission possible. Review the mission statement so that you understand each facet of our mission. This process is best started by becoming spiritually aware of what God is doing in our midst and determining how we can join Him in His efforts. The budget process is not an isolated business process devoid of spiritual perception; we have been gifted to do ministry in His name with those resources. He has privileged us to be stewards of it. It might be wise to have a visioning meeting with your organization to allow members to express their views.

EXAMPLE: Suppose you represent the Stewardship Committee and need to prepare a budget request for the coming year. What is your part in the mission of the church? A statement might be: "The Stewardship Committee strives to make all church members aware of the talents and resources of which we have been gifted and maximize the use of those resources so that the church can achieve the mission set out before use."

II. What the objectives that your organization wishes to accomplish in the next fiscal year? Some of those objectives may be stand alone objectives and others may be continuations of objectives begun in previous years. Each objective must be tied directly back to part of the mission statement; if it cannot then we don't need to be doing it.

EXAMPLE: *The Stewardship Committee then must determine what objects it wishes to accomplish during the next year. One objective might be "to make every church member aware of how his or her money is being used to forward the spread of the Gospel around the world." This enhances our participation in evangelism and provides opportunities for reaching others with the Gospel message. Although this directly deals with learning (discipleship) it promotes witnessing (evangelism). Another objective might be "to determine the spiritual resources within the church so that those resources might be cultivated and enabled." Such resources include spiritual gifts, talents, inclinations, and material wealth.*

III. What must the organization and church do to accomplish these objectives? Define a course of action to implement your concept..

EXAMPLE: *The Stewardship Committee has developed the following action plans to achieve these objectives. First, the church will hold a Stewardship Fair in the month of April to learn how church funds are being used. Also, guest speakers will be solicited from supported agencies and organizations to share their successes and needs. A second action plan might include the use of surveys and tests to discern giftedness and interests among the membership.*

PROPOSED BUDGET

ORGANIZATION	ORIGINAL REQUEST	NEGOTIATED REQUEST	FINAL ALLOCATION

INSTRUCTIONS

During the budget workshop it will be necessary to keep track of changes to the budgets of various organizations. This form provides an easy method of listing changes to various budget requests.

Budget Request Form

NO: _____   Fiscal Year: _____

This form is to be completed by departmental and ministry leaders on an annual basis to request funding on The Church Budget. Complete form in its entirety.

Today's Date: _____   Your Name & Ministry/Dept.: _____
Daytime Telephone#: _____   Email Address: _____

DEPARTMENTAL/MINISTRY PARTNER

Sub-Department of: _____
Department Dir. _____

AMOUNT BUDGETED LAST FY: _____
AMOUNT OF EXPENSES YTD: _____
AMOUNT REQUESTED FOR FY: ___ : $

Itemize your expected expenses as much as possible.

_____	$
_____	$
_____	$
_____	$
_____	$
_____	$
_____	$
_____	$
_____	$
_____	$
_____	$
_____	$
_____	$
_____	$
_____	$
_____	$
_____	$
_____	$
_____	$
_____	$
_____	$

Continue on page 2 for additional itemization.

TOTAL FROM PAGE 2 $ _____

Miscellaneous/Other Supplies $ _____

TOTAL AMOUNT REQUESTED $_____

After prayerfully considering the needs of the ministry of department in which I serve at _____. I submit to The Church my requests.

_____
Signature of Department/Ministry Leader   Date Signed

_____
Signature of Department Chair   Date Signed

What is the mission statement/plan of your ministry or department for the next fiscal year (be specific, list goals and initiatives you plan to achieve)?

_____
_____
_____
_____

Continue on page 2, if needed.
Please share these thoughts with the member of your ministry.

IMPORTANT CONSIDERATIONS

-The Church Budget is comprised of the requests of ministry and departmental leaders. The leaders are considered to_____ Budget Committee, and The Church must approve The Church Budget on an annual basis.

-The Church Budget is more than just a set of numbers relating to the expenses of particular depts.. The Church Budget is the annual mission plan for the church and is one of the most important documents at _____. We hope you prepare your request prayerfully and thoughtfully to best carryout your particular ministry/department's mission.

-Please think ahead. Throughout each year you should begin compiling a list of expenditures in which your department will require for the next fiscal year.

-**Please complete this form and deliver it to the church office no later than __Nov. 22nd___. If the church office is not in receipt of the request by the time mentioned above. Your Ministry/Department may suffer from not being budgeted or may be placed under the direction of the church office.**

-This form may be completed online at _____ and/or emailed to _____

-If you have any questions, please feel free to contact _____

Church Office Use Only   ____NEW

Received on _____ by _____
Account Codes _____
Church Name: _____
Church Treasurer: _____

B-29

Budget Request Form (Page 2)

Mission Statement Continued from Page 1: _____
_____
_____
_____
_____

Expected expense itemized (continued from P1):	
_____	$
_____	$
_____	$
_____	$
_____	$
_____	$
_____	$
_____	$
_____	$
_____	$
_____	$
_____	$
_____	$
_____	$
_____	$
_____	$
_____	$
_____	$
_____	$
_____	$
_____	$
_____	$
_____	$
_____	$
_____	$

Enter the total amount of this list to the list on Page 1.

PAGE 2 TOTAL $_____

Office Use Only:

Initials of Department/Ministry Leader AND Department Chair:

_____   _____

Page 2

Church Name: _____
Church Address: _____
City, State Zip: _____
Church Treasurer: _____

Proposed Church Planting Budget Worksheet
For Fiscal Year 20___

New Church Name:

Pastor's Name:

INCOME PROJECTIONS (first year) $_____

101 Tithes and Offerings (contribution income) _____
102 Association and Denominational Support _____
103 Partnering Church Support _____
104 New Work Support Raised by Planter and Staff _____
105 Rental Facility Contributions _____
106 Interests on Checking/Savings Accounts _____
107 Other _____

> **Total Projected Income _____**
> **Average Monthly Income Needed _____**

Income Dispersements (first year)

CHURCH STAFF

201 Planter's Salary _____
202 Planter's Moving Expense _____
203 Planter's Housing and Utilities Allowance _____
204 Planter's Health Insurance _____
205 Planter's Annuity _____
206 Planter's Travel Expense Reimbursement
        (_____¢ per mile up to _____ miles/year) _____
207 Ministerial Retreat Expenses _____
208 Planter's Social Security Allowance and Other Benefits _____
209 Church Office Secretary's Salary _____
210 Payroll Expenses (federal and state taxes) _____
211 Worker's Compensation Premiums _____

MINISTRY EXPENSES

301 Advertising (direct mail, telemarketing, etc.) _____
302 Promotional Literature and Printing _____
303 Postage _____
304 Office Supplies _____
305 Office and Computer Equipment/Software/etc._____
306 Telephone/Internet _____
307 Worship Ministries and Copyright Licenses _____
308 Evangelism and Ministry Training _____
309 Christian Education and Discipleship/Small Groups _____
310 Leadership and Teacher Training _____
311 New Member Training _____
312 Children's and Youth Ministry _____
313 Hospitality and Fellowship Ministries _____
314 Other _____

NORTH AMERICA AND WORLD MISSIONS

401 Local Association and Denominational Cooperative Program
Participation (Assoc. 3%)_____ (C.P. 10%) _____
402 Local Compassion & Kindness Ministries _____
403 Daughter Church Fund (for future church plants from our church)
_____
404 Other _____

FACILITIES

501 Meeting Place, Office and Storage Rental/Lease _____
502 Maintenance (buildings and grounds) _____
503 Property and Liability Insurance _____
504 Meeting Place Utilities _____
505 Equipment (instruments, sound, lights, transportation, etc.)
_____
506 Legal Fees _____
507 Building Fund Savings _____
508 Other _____

Total Projected Expenses _____

Average Monthly Expenses _____

[Church Name]
Fundraiser Accounting Form

Please complete and distribute this form BEFORE your event (with estimates only) and AFTER your event (same form as estimates, but include actuals) to: _____

Name of Event: _____   Date of Event: _____

Account/Club Name: _____   Account Number: _____

Event Leader/Contact Information: _____

Fundraised monies will be used for: _____

_____

	ESTIMATE (Before)	ACTUAL (After)
A - Number of items to be purchased/expected attendees:	_____	_____
B - Cost per items/person:	_____	_____
C - **Total Cost (A x B):**	_____	_____
D - Number of items to be sold/expected attendees:	_____	_____
E - Cost per items/person:	_____	_____
F - **Total Revenue (D x E):**	_____	_____
G – Revenue (Line F)	_____	_____
H - Cost (Line C)	_____	_____
I - **Profit**	_____	_____

Explanation of difference between estimate and actual profit: _____

_____

Approval of Fundraiser (BEFORE the event):

_____   _____
Event Organizer   Date

_____   _____
Department Chair or Club Advisor   Date

_____   _____
Division Director of Fundraiser Activities   Date

Approval of Actuals (AFTER the event):

_____   _____
Department Chair or Club Advisor   Date

_____   _____
Division Director of Fundraiser Activities   Date

ALL deposits for this event should contain the same description as above.   B-33

[Church Name]
Fundraising Accounting Form

Name of Event: _____

Organizing Group/Ministry: _____

Event Leader/Contact Information: _____

_____

Date of Event: _____

Estimated # of Participants/Attendees: _____

Number of Event Volunteers: _____

Estimated # of Volunteer Hours: _____

INCOME Details (e.g. ticket sales, food, silent auction, etc.):

_____   _____

_____   _____

_____   _____

_____   **TOTAL INCOME:** _____

Estimated Value of Any **Non-Cash Donations** (Please detail # of items, quantity):
(Please do not add this estimate to Total Income.)

_____   _____

_____   _____

_____   _____

_____   _____

EXPENSE Details (e.g. food, equipment rental, supplies, postage, etc.):

_____   _____

_____   _____

_____   _____

_____   **TOTAL EXPENSES:** _____

                                        NET EVENT PROCEEDS (Income – Expenses):

                                        _____

Form completed by: _____   Date: _____

_____ CHURCH

Physical Inventory Count Sheet

Sheet # _____

Location _____

Item Number	Description	Quantity	Location

Counted by _____ Date _____

CHURCH INVENTORY LIST

Copy a sheet for each room/area in the church; use more than one sheet if needed.

_____   _____   _____
Sheet #   Room #, Name or Area   Use of Room/Area

General contents of room/area:

_____

_____

_____

Specific equipment/property to be noted:

Item(s) Name	Brief Description	Model / Serial Number	Approx-imate Age	Estim-ated Value	Notes

Inventory completed by:

_____

CHURCH FACILITIES SURVEY

	Superior	Adequate	Inadequate	Unacceptable	Remarks
Sanctuary					
Pews					
Pulpit furniture					
Sound					
Lighting					
Paint					
Floor covering					
Maintenance					
Halls					
Stairs					
Lighting					
Paint					
Floor covering					
Maintenance					
Restrooms					
Fixtures					
Lighting					
Paint					
Floor covering					
Maintenance					
Departments					
Equipment					
Storage					
Lighting					
Paint					
Floor covering					
Maintenance					
Classrooms					
Equipment					
Lighting					
Paint					
Floor covering					
Maintenance					

1

CHURCH FACILITIES SURVEY

	Superior	Adequate	Inadequate	Unacceptable	Remarks
Kitchen/Dining					
Storage					
Paint					
Floor covering					
Maintenance					
Appliances					
Utilities					
Heating					
Air conditioning					
Plumbing					
Electrical					
Offices					
Storage					
Lighting					
Paint					
Floor covering					
Maintenance					
Building Exterior					
Paint					
Roof					
Windows & Doors					
Steps					
Grounds					
Lawn					
Landscaping					
Sidewalks					
Maintenance					
Lighting					
Parking					

CHURCH FACILITIES SURVEY

	Superior	Adequate	Inadequate	Unacceptable	Remarks
Signs					
Welcoming visitors					
Basic information					
Directions to office					
Directions to S. School					
Directions to worship					
Handicap Services					
Convenient Parking					
Ramps					
Access to sanctuary					
Bathroom facilities					
Other					

Church Bylaws - Sample:

By-Laws of [church]

ARTICLE I – PRINCIPAL OFFICE

The principal office of the corporation, (also referred to as the Ministry) shall be located at: [Address, City, State Zip]

ARTICLE II – STRUCTURE OF MINISTRY, CIVIL, AND ECCLESIASTICAL

2.1 Civil Structure. The civil officers of the corporation may be a President, Vice-President, Director of Spiritual Innovation, Secretary, Treasurer, and such other offices as the corporation shall establish. (You may put in whatever offices you like, as long as you have a President and a Treasurer.)

2.1.1 The President shall be the Pastor and shall preside at all meetings and shall make an annual report to the status and condition of the corporation to this Board of Directors. The President shall sign all certificates, contracts, deeds and other instruments of the corporation. During the absence or disability of the President, the Vice-President shall exercise all the powers and discharge all the duties of the President.

2.1.2 The Director of Spiritual Innovation shall exercise creative input on the spiritual content of the church material and shall be diligent to the act of improving the overall teaching standards of the church.

2.1.3 The Secretary shall keep the minutes of all meetings: shall have charge of the seal and corporate books and shall make such reports and reform such duties as are required of him or her by the corporation, and shall sign all certificates, contracts, deeds and other instruments of the corporation.

2.1.4 The Treasurer shall have custody of all monies and securities of the corporation and shall keep regular books of account. He or she shall disburse the funds of the corporation in payment of the just demands against the corporation or as may be required of him/her he/she shall make an accounting of all his transactions as Treasurer and of the financial condition of the corporation.

2.1.5 The officers of the corporation shall hold offices until their successors are duly elected and qualified.

2.1.6 The Board of Directors shall meet at least once each year, either in person or electronically, but special meetings may be called if and when the same may become necessary.

2.2 Ecclesiastical Structure. Ecclesiastically, the Ministry shall be composed of:

2.2.1 The Board of Directors

ARTICLE III – THE BOARD OF DIRECTORS, ITS ORGANIZATION, POWERS AND DUTIES

3.1 The Board of Directors shall be at least 3 in number and shall have the power to exercise all powers necessary for the operation of the Ministry, expressed or implied, which shall be necessary and proper to carry out all the executive functions, and all other powers both civil and ecclesiastical as it may determine.

3.1.1 The members of the Board of Directors shall be elected for a term of 5 years. The Terms shall be computed from the day of their election and each member may hold office until such time as an election by the members can he had.

3.1.2 In the event of vacancy in the Board of Directors occurs, remaining members of the Board of Directors shall fill such vacancy by a majority vote at a duly held meeting until the successor has been duly elected and qualified.

3.2 The Pastor. The Pastor may be the President and may be appointed by the Board of Directors, which shall authorize the Pastor and any other officers, or agents of the Ministry, or any other officer so authorized by these Bylaws, to enter into any contract or execute and deliver any instrument in the name of or on behalf of the Ministry, and such authority may be general or may be confined to specific incidence.

3.3 The Secretary. The Secretary shall be elected by the Board of Directors or appointed by the President.

3.3.1 The Secretary shall keep minutes of the proceedings of its members, Board of Directors, committees, councils and other Boards or tribunals authorized by the Board of Directors and these records shall be kept at the principal office of the Ministry.

3.4 The Treasurer. The Treasurer shall be elected by the Board of Directors or appointed by the President. The Treasurer shall be the treasurer of the Ministry, and shall have custody of all monies and securities of the Ministry and shall make an accounting of all the Ministry transactions.

3.4.1 All checks, drafts or orders for the payment of money, notes , evidence of indebtedness issued in the name of the corporation shall be signed by the Pastor or other officers or agents of the corporation, in such manner as shall from time to time be determined by resolution of the Board of Directors. In the absence of such direction from the Board of Directors the Pastor may sign on behalf of the Ministry.

3.4.2 All funds of the Ministry shall be deposited as required to the credit of the corporation in such banks, trust companies or other depositories as the Board of Directors or the Pastor may elect.

3.4.3 The Board of Directors or the Pastor may accept on behalf of the Ministry any contributions, donations, gifts, including real property, bequest or devise for any purpose of the Ministry. (Malachi 3:10; Luke 6:38; I Corinthians 16:1; I Corinthians 9:6-8).

3.4.4 The Treasurer shall keep correct and complete financial records of all Ministry account(s). All books and records of the Ministry may be inspected by any member, or agent, for any purpose at any reasonable time.

3.4.5 The treasurer shall be authorized to appoint personals to assist the Treasurer in carrying out the duties and functions of the Treasurer's Office.

ARTICLE IV – MEETINGS

4.1 The annual meeting of the Ministry shall be held on the first Tuesday of May of each year. At that meeting Directors shall be nominated and elected to office as appropriate.

4.2 Special Meetings may be called by the Board of Directors or the Pastor as they in their discretion deem necessary. Notices for the calling of such special meetings shall be given to all members in writing with 3 days prior written notice.

ARTICLE V – RULES AND REGULATIONS

5.1 The Board of Directors may adopt such rules of procedure and regulations governing the conduct of its business and the organization of the Ministry as they may deem necessary, proper and expedient.

5.1.1 There can be no appeal from the decisions and determinations of the Board of Directors.

ARTICLE VI – AMENDMENTS TO THE BYLAWS

The provisions of the Bylaws may be modified, altered, or amended by two-thirds majority vote of the members of the Board of Directors at a regular or special meeting. As soon as the proposed amendments have been adopted as herein provided, results of the vote shall be announced by the Pastor and declared adopted by the Chairman of the Board of Directors, whereupon such amendments shall be in full force of effect.

IN WITNESS WHEREOF, I have hereunto set my hand and seal, acknowledged and filed the foregoing Articles of Incorporation under the laws of the State of [State] this _____ day of [Month], [Year].

_____, Incorporator
Signature of Incorporator

_____
Print Name of Incorporator

[Church Name]

[Church Address]

BUSINESS PLAN 20__ (SAMPLE)

[Church Website]

Purpose of the Project

To create a welcoming environment for a wider range of community activities and users at [Church Name] by:
- Improving accessibility into and around the building for all current and potential users from the local community.
- Creating a flexible space suitable for a wide variety of community uses and worship.
- Maximizing available space and minimizing health and safety risks.
- Improving the toilet facilities including those provided to meet the needs of the disabled;
- Reducing the cost and environmental impact of our heating system.

1

Table of Contents

Church Location & Background

[Church Name] is a village at [Church Location], which was once a rural village but with the developments during the last century is now an urban area adjoining the City of [Name of City]. The population of [City] is approximately [Population#].

[You can insert pictures of the church here and even a map to the church if you want.]

The existing church premises, built in 1900 have served the community well. There have been subsequent improvements with a hall added to the rear in the 1970s, but a major refurbishment is required to ensure the premises meet legislative requirements and are appropriate for the needs of present and future generations of the community and the mission of the church.

[You can insert pictures of the church here.]

The central heating boiler installed in the 70s was connected to the existing pipe work within the existing church, which has a sloped and stepped floor. The rear hall has a stepped, narrow entrance and corridors to the rest of the building. To accommodate all potential users the improvements need to take account of compliance with the Disability Discrimination Act. We have a membership of [Membership#] with [# of Regular Worshippers] regular worshippers.

Use of the Building and Public Access

The general public, either individually or a group may have access to the building by booking in advance. Details of how to make a booking are displayed on the church premises.

On a regular basis the premises are in use as follows:

Sunday	10:00 – 12:00 - Morning Service with Coffee Followed by Refreshments
	10:30 – 11:30 – Junior Church
	18:00 – 19:30 – Evening Service
	20:00 – 21:00 – After 8 Service led by the Young People (Bi-Monthly)
Monday	19:30 – 21:00 – Wesley Guild (Oct – Apr)
Tuesday	10:30 – 11:30 – Men's Fellowship (Monthly)
	14:00 – 15:00 – Friendly Hour
	20:00 – 21:30 – Music Group
Wednesday	18:00 – 19:30 – Evening Service
	20:00 – 21:30 – Women's Circle (Bi-Weekly)
Thursday	12:00 – 13:00 – *Luncheon Club
Friday	13:00 – 15:00 – Jumble Sale (Bi-Monthly)
	19:00 – 19:30 – Prayer Fellowship (Monthly)
Saturday	10:10 – 12:00 – Coffee Mornings (Bi-Monthly)

Most mid-week events are attended by members of the community as well as church members.
*Luncheon club is for elderly people living alone within the community, to have a meal together.

Current Number of Users

Group	Number and Frequency
Wesley Guild	25 Predominantly Church (Weekly – October – April)
Men's Fellowship	16: 10 Church, 6 Community (Monthly)
Friendly Hour	56: 18 Church, 38 Community (Weekly)
Music Group	11 Church
Women's Circle	15 of which 4 Church and 11 Community (Fortnightly)
Luncheon Club	30 Helpers (14 Church, 16 Community) on a Rota, 36 Diners (Elderly people living alone within the community) some coming weekly, others fortnightly.
Jumble Sales	Held to raise money to run the church minibus, which is used by the church to bring people to meetings (predominantly Friendly Hour) and by community groups, e.g. scouts (bi-monthly).
Prayer Fellowship	8 Church (Monthly)
Coffee Mornings	Held not only to raise money, but to provide a meeting place with cake & usually a car wash which especially older people appreciate (bi-monthly).

After 8 Service	A restaurant-style service organized and led by the young people of the church, with video clips, music group and guest speaker, up to 70 attend with a good proportion from outside the church (bi-monthly).

As well as the above we also hold an annual Christmas tree festival, where local businesses, groups and individuals can sponsor a tree. This is held from Friday to Monday at the beginning of advent and is enjoyed by the local community young and hold with approximately 400 visitors, entrance if free.

[Church Name]

Our **Mission** as the [Church Name] in [City] is called by Christ to be:

*A Welcoming Community   *A Witnessing Community   *A Worshipping Community

Our **Vision** is to Worship God as known in Jesus, seek His will and draw those around into a relationship with Him.

Our **value** is to reflect on and test our heritage as [Church Doctrine]

Our **strategy** is to:
- Offer the opportunity for people of all ages to grow in faith and in discipleship.
- Offer an open community which values every individual.
- Identify and try to meet the needs of the local community.
- Offer a safe space for all.
- Work in partnership with other groups in the community as appropriate.
- Work in partnership with other local churches whenever possible.

Achieving our Strategy

In [Year] it became increasingly apparent that the premises no longer were sufficient to meet increased numbers and growing demand. Also the lack of a safe space, adequate heating, restricted disabled access throughout, compliance with health and safety regulations and the need to reduce our carbon footprint led the Property Committee to propose three alternative plans to meet current and foreseeable demand. These were presented to a General Church Meeting in [Date of Meeting].

To date this has been achieved through:
- Comments sought from members and existing user groups.
- Consultation with outside user groups – ongoing.
- Consultation with the local community – ongoing.
- A dreaming dreams day – what the people would like to see happen in the church in the next 3 to 5 years.
- TRIO (The Responsibility is Ours) – a program to challenge people about responsible giving.
- Appointment of a part-time (20 hours per week) lay worker.
- Various community events, e.g. Annual Community Christmas Tree Festival, Coffee Mornings.
- Lettings coordinator – more interactive than previous including promotion of community facilities.

The result of consultations were discussed with the architect who has produced a feasibility cost budget within which, inclusive of professional fees and VAT, all the envisaged works will be contained.

Meanwhile, church members, user groups and community contacts are working together to achieve our values and objectives to ensure systems are in place to properly manage and sustain the improved facilities when they become available by:

- Promoting our plans through community publications such as Faith Link, local newspaper and radio.
- Publicizing the improved facilities to the local authorities, social services, etc.
- Development of website.
- Management and Communications Team – Monitor progress and feedback on a regular basis.
- Fundraising Team – Internal.
- Grants Team – External Funders.

This refurbishment and improvement scheme aims to achieve our objective of providing safe accessible space and facilities for as wide as possible a cross section of the community.

Identification of the Need for the Improvement of Facilities

Background

The premises have been kept in a good state of repair and improvements have been made in providing disabled facilities under the direction of the Property Committee and Church Council. However, the Property Committee of [Church Name] has identified over a number of years the necessity for further upgrading of the premises, in particular the heating system. This has been backed up by issues highlighted in the [Church Name]'s Quinqennial Review.

The issues identified as a particular necessity were:

- Ramp with a more suitable degree of slope for disabled access
- Disabled toilet with easy wheelchair access
- Visibility of the rear entrance to users of the building
- Removal of the sloping floor of the sanctuary
- Removal of the stepped entrance to the rear hall
- Removal of the narrow corridors to the rear hall
- New heating system to reduce the churches carbon footprint
- Convert the existing sanctuary into a large multipurpose venue equipped with multimedia facilities there by increasing the range of options for community use
- Replace crumbling stone window sills
- Improve ventilation
- Rebuild crumbling boundary wall
- Increase the available space for children's and young people's work
- Eliminate overcrowding in the premises and improve overall safety
- Provide a storage area for equipment

Description of the Site

[Church Name] premises consist of an outside area comprising a small off-street car parking area (space for four or five cars) and grassed area with access down both sides of the building. A sloping ramp provides access to the front porch. The main worship area has a sloping floor with side aisles and fixed rows of pews, plus a number of movable chairs. Partitioned off to one side is a small meeting room which leads to a vestry and office area, with the photocopier occupying an area inside the side porch. Doors lead through to a larger back room with a kitchen area to one side and doors to the two toilets and the side entrance at the other side.

The worship area is used regularly for Sunday services (morning and evening) and Wednesday evening services, and also for weddings, funerals and christenings. This area has most recently been the venue for restaurant-style After 8 services which are led by the young people in the church and have attracted 40+ people.

The vestry is used as the church office, a storage facility and for the preacher on Sundays and Wednesdays before services.

The small meeting room is used when the congregation needs to spill over from the main worship area by pulling back the partition. It is also used after the service on a Sunday morning for refreshments – there is a serving hatch from the kitchen. This room is also used for meetings such as the Property Committee and could hold about 24 seated around tables.

The kitchen was refurbished in 1996 and is fitted to a high standard with steel work surfaces, a commercial cooker, dishwasher, sinks and has serving hatches to the other rooms. It is used regularly for the preparation of refreshments, most significantly for the serving of about 24 meals for the Luncheon Club.

The rear hall is used on Sunday mornings for Junior Church, plush other weekday meetings. The luncheon Club and Friendly Hour meetings use it to its fullest capacity.

Scheme Objectives

The building alterations and refurbishment of [Church Name] will make the premises:

- Safer
- More Accessible for all Users
- More Comfortable
- More Flexible
- More Attractive

Overall the scheme will:

- Give Added Value to Users
- Offer a more Attractive Modern Option to Users
- Provide a new Lease of Life to a well-used Community Facility
- Offer a Flexible Space to Attract More Users
- Ensure the Previses are a Continued Community Asset for the Future
- Increase the Range of Community Services the Church is able to Provide
- Assist the Church to Achieve its Mission, Vision and Calling

The scheme will provide the following specific outputs:

- Welcoming New Front Entrance with Easy Disabled Access
- Refurbished Worship Area with Flexibility to be Used for many other Purposes during the Week
- Level Floor in the Worship Area
- Fully DDA Compliant Disabled Toilet
- New Accessible and Visible Rear Entrance to the Premises
- New Storage Facilities for all Users
- New Church Office
- New Church Vestry
- New Environmentally Friendly Heating System
- Modern Presentation Equipment and Audio System

The outputs will achieve the following:

- Accessibility for all Users Including Wheelchairs, Pushchairs and Prams
- Improved Building Security and Child Protection
- Safe and Comfortable Toilet Facilities for all Users
- A much more Flexible and Safer Space for use by the Community
- A warm Welcoming Building with Reduced Environmental Impact

Details of the Project

[Insert pictures of what is being discussed below.]

The ramp to the front entrance will be removed and the front doors replaced with glass doors improving the access and make the building more welcoming.

The side entrance to the building will be removed and replaced with a new entrance which will face down the long path which gives access to it.

Both of the new entrances will be fully DDA compliant.

Current Main Worship Area

[Insert pictures of what is being discussed below.]

The worship area currently has a mixture of mainly fixed wooden pews and some moveable seating at the front. To the left front of the worship area is a small meeting room which is separated from the worship area by a folding wooden screen. The floor of the worship area slopes from the back of the front and the aisles at each side of the pews are narrow.

[Insert pictures of what is being discussed below.]

As part of the project all the pews will be removed as will the sloping floor. The floor will be leveled to the same height as the new front entrance doors giving easy access to the front of the building. This will create a large multipurpose flexible space suitable for many groups.

Office Space

[Insert pictures of what is being discussed below.]

The current vestry duels as an office and is unsuitable at present for both purposes. The entrance to the rear meeting room involves passing through several doors to gain access to the room itself and the toilets.

Rear Meeting Room

[Insert pictures of what is being discussed below.]

The project will result in the rear of the premises being altered to improve the access from the side entrance door (see above) by creating a new extension which will include the new side entrance and vestibule, make the current disabled toilet fully DDA complaint and separate office and vestry. This will also result in the moving of one of the existing toilets and the some of the many doors accessing the rear meeting room.

Toilet Facilities

[Insert pictures of what is being discussed below.]

There are currently two toilets (on the left) in the building which are accessed via a narrow corridor which gives restricted access for both disabled and wheelchair users. One of the current toilets has some disabled facilities but it is not DDA compliant and access is difficult.

The new extension will incorporate the moving of one of the existing toilets and the narrow corridor as part of the rear extension giving far better access to the disabled toilet which will be made fully DDA complaint. (see plan)

Audio and Visual Aids

The worship area currently has an audio system with hearing aid loop which was installed approximately 15 years ago. The system is now showing signs of its age and is no longer fit for purpose. There is currently no built in visual aids systems.

As part of the project a new and more flexible audio system will be installed including a loop system along with a modern visual aids/presentation system for use by all users including Sunday and Wednesday Worship.

Future Management of the Premises

The premises will continue to be managed by the [Church Name] Council with assistance and information being offered by Church Stewards and the church members.

The [Church Name] will continue to oversee the running of the Church in accordance with the rules, principles and values of the [Church Name].

Track Record of Delivering Projects

The management of all [Church Name] building schemes is overseen by Local, District and National governing bodies. Those involved at the District and National level have expertise and experience in overseeing building projects.

Local [Church] building schemes require the approval of district and national bodies who employ and use relevant professionals to examine and check all schemes prior to approval. Their advice is available throughout the project.

The church premises in [City] having been operating on the site since 1900 and have undergone many changes and improvements. The most recent was in 1996 when a new kitchen was built and the front entrance altered to give improved access including a ramp for wheelchair users. There have also been several minor schemes over the last few years including the alternation of the toilets to give improved disabled access and relaying of the block flooring in the large meeting room.

The premises are managed by the Church Council through delegated powers given to the Property Committee who oversee all of the upkeep and maintenance of the premises.

Due to the successful use of the premises as a church and a community facility we have reached the stage where we need to modernize and develop the premises further in order to open up the building to wider use by providing a flexible multipurpose space.

Summary

The improvements to the premises will not only maintain the church building but will also enable the premises to be made available to a wider section of the community due to the flexibility and improved access that the scheme will offer.

The scheme will also make the building safer, more accessible and useable to all members of the community from the very young to the very old.

The churches environmental footprint will be greatly reduced by the installation of a new energy efficient heating system.

The scheme will undoubtedly improve the facilities available and contribute to the ongoing task of developing a dynamic and caring community in the local area.

[Insert a full picture of the front of the church here.]

Timeline of Development of Scheme

October 20__   The church agreed to look at how we might update and adapt the premises to make them more user friendly, and to appoint an architect to see what is structurally possible.

Spring 20__   Architect appointed and a plan of what would be possible structurally with the oldest part of the building.

May 20__   Fundraising launched.

Spring 20__   Three sets of plans presented to the church based on the original structural possibility plan.

Summer 20__   After consultation with members, it was decided the plans did not address the main short comings with the building, and alternative proposals were agreed.

Spring 20__   Planning permission obtained.

Summer 20__   Detailed plans received from the architect in line with the Summer 20__ proposals, these were agreed with an alteration to the interior layout.

November 20__   Went out to the tender.

January 20__   Tenders received.

Management and Appraisal of the Scheme

The scheme is managed by the Church Property Committee consisting of:

[Committee Member's Name], Property Secretary and Steward, an insurance claims handler
[Committee Member's Name], Property Chair and Steward, an accountant
[Committee Member's Name], Church Treasurer, a retired health visitor
[Committee Member's Name], Senior Church Steward, a semi-retired paramedic

In addition, [Architect's Name and Company Name] is our architect.

The progress of the scheme is evaluated by the Church Council at regular intervals, chair the [Rev. Name]

The [Church] property office scrutinizes and evaluates the schemes technical aspects, its objectives and the financial requirements/implications and advises as necessary.

66696814R00054

Made in the USA
Lexington, KY
21 August 2017